The Money Guide to Transform your Life

About the Author

Lynn Beattie (previously James) is a personal finance expert and founder of Mrs MummyPenny. Her background is a CIMA management accountant of 17 years with a breath of experience working in commercial finance for Tesco, EE & HSBC. She is a single mum to three boys, living in Hertfordshire.

She left the corporate world in 2015 to run Mrs Mummypenny full-time. She writes about personal finance with a healthy wealth, body and mind angle.

Lynn features regularly on campaigns for PensionBee, Aldi, LifeSearch & Zopa Bank. Also featuring regularly in the media including The Financial Times, The Sun, iWeekend, ITV and BBC TV/Radio. She presents a weekly Podcast/YouTube show, Mrs MummyPenny Talks.

This is her second printed book. The first, Blogging Your Way to Riches published in 2017.

The Money Guide to Transform your Life

by

Lynn Beattie

To my mum

Contents

The Future – Part 2

Foreword from Romi Savova

How can you make the most of your money? Families around the country - and especially women, who often take on the lion's share of household financial planning - are asking themselves this very question at a time when future economic prospects are increasingly uncertain.

Financial freedom gives people the power to pursue their dreams, to live a happier life and to have more meaningful relationships. Yet many of us struggle to achieve it. People often manage money in flight mode: we buy what we need (and want), pay our bills, take on debt we think we can afford, and save where we can. Navigating the financial system as a consumer is complicated - there are entire sections in our major newspapers dedicated to the things that could go wrong. And talking about money is still taboo. Families, personal experiences and our life choices are all intertwined with our spending habits.

The Money Guide to Transform Your Life is a deeply personal and brave account of Lynn's journey towards financial freedom. It is a rare glimpse into the life events that shape people, and ultimately their approaches to money. Lynn's story from childhood and the loss of two parents to building a successful business, while being a single mum to three boys, will inspire you to make better decisions about your own finances.

The Money Guide to Transform Your Life offers a blueprint for managing money effectively and with intent. The book is chock full with practical, first-hand and hard-learned tips. It is an engaging and devourable explanation of how to budget, how to do the weekly shop and how to enjoy holidays without the subsequent guilt trip. The Money Guide to Transform Your Life will demystify savings, including the all-necessary emergency fund, and of course the long-term benefits of pensions, the topic closest to my own heart. With a little effort, this book can save you money right now, help you get out of debt, build up a nest egg for retirement and get you in control of your finances.

Mrs. MummyPenny, the brand, is a humorous play on Lynn's own role as mother and household financial administrator. Its effectiveness stems from the recognition that purposeful money management is intimately linked to the life moments and experiences that make us laugh, that make us angry, happy, sad and everything in between. If you are reading this foreword, then you too must be ready to transform your life, to take the road towards financial freedom and to be your very own (financial) hero. Cheers to that!

Romi Savova is Chief Executive Officer of PensionBee, the leading online pension provider she founded to simplify pension savings in the UK, following a harrowing pension transfer experience of her own. PensionBee uses technology to help customers combine their old pensions into one new online plan. PensionBee customers can see their live balance, make contributions and withdrawals online and use a smart calculator to plan their saving. We are a proud partner to Mrs MummyPenny and delighted that Lynn has chosen PensionBee as her pension provider.

Why should you read another book about money?

There's no escaping the importance of money. We need it to function in everyday life. Money has a kind of power associated with it. It can control us and in doing so, put us out of control of our own lives. Nobody wants that.

Since starting my money blogging business Mrs MummyPenny nearly ten years ago I've become increasingly aware of a certain kind of poverty in the UK: it is a poverty of access to financial education and knowledge. It is a poverty that most impacts women and minority groups, and it is one that I have made it my mission to help end.

My goal is for every woman to have financial understanding and freedom. In reading this book you'll have access to the tools and the confidence you need to manage your money now and in the future. What could be more transformative?

My book is split into two parts. I open Part 1 with the story of my life, revealing how several massive events have shaped my relationship with money in different ways, some good, many bad. I do this to show the extent to which our relationship with money is emotional, it is part of who we are and not something rational and objective. Understanding that through the lens of my story will hopefully help you to see your own relationship with money in a new and potentially revolutionary light. Part 1 goes on to cover short-term personal finance, everyday management that many women must do and figure out for themselves. I talk budgeting, money saving on household bills, food, family time, healthy body and mind. I also talk debt repayment and making money.

Each chapter is packed full of real-life experience from me, guidance and tools to help you manage your day-to-day, month-to-month money better. There are useful exercises for you to complete at your own pace. I've structured the book in such a way to enable you to either pick it up and put it down after each chapter, or read the whole book in one go.

Part 2 is about medium- to long-term finance. In this section I walk you through the tools that can help guide you towards financial freedom. There are chapters on wills, insurance, savings, investing, pensions and setting up your own business. I have made LOTS of mistakes through life with these finance areas, and I don't hold back in revealing some of the messy places I've landed. We are all human. If there's a better place to learn from than mistakes, I don't know about it. Though if by sharing mine, I can save you from making the same ones that would be a real success in my mind!

I end my book with a chapter called "Do What Makes You Happy". I am a firm believer in combining your life passion with your career. Whatever you are passionate about in your personal life, if you can turn this into your job as well? What an incredible life achievement.

I made a promise to make my book fun, to make you laugh and possibly make cry. Most importantly, you will be guided and inspired to change your financial habits for the better.

PART 1 – THE NOW

Chapter 1 – My Story

How we behave with our money today, right now, is a direct product of who we are, where we've come from and the lessons we've learned (or not!) along the journey. In the coming chapters I will help you to navigate your own financial history, thus enabling you to become more economically empowered.

Whilst I've always been good with numbers and financially astute on paper, I know that the emotional challenges I have faced have dictated the way I have responded to and managed money. Getting real about your relationship with money, understanding the roots of that relationship, is key to transforming where you go from here in your money management. My intention is that, in sharing my story, you can start to see more clearly how your story has influenced your current approach to money. From that clear vantage point, with support from this guide, you can reassert control over this important force in our lives.

Early Money Memories

I grew up in Penzance, Cornwall with my mum and dad. I was a joyful gift to them in their 40s. They had already brought up my sister and brother in the 1950's and 1960's whilst dad was in the army and learnt from their mistakes. By the 1970s they had settled in Cornwall in a granite built terraced house in Penzance town centre. My bedroom was in the attic with glorious views over Mounts Bay and St. Michaels Mount. My mum loved me so much, so much that she didn't want to send me to nursery, she wanted to keep me at home for as long as possible, just the two of us.

My earliest memories of money are linked to independence and me being given the freedom to learn and understand money and maths.

One of my first toys was a Fisher-Price School house with magnetic numbers and alphabet. I loved learning - sums, and words, but mostly sums.

From the age of six I was responsible for counting the money my dad saved in special silver tankards kept high up on our dresser. Dad and I would take the bagged up money to the Bradford and Bingley Building society where I'd watch mesmerised as the cashiers re-counted and banked the pennies. It wasn't long before I opened my first account, becoming the proud owner of an account passbook in which they would write (yes, write) the amount I was paying in or taking out and update the balance with interest added. I loved looking at the changing numbers in that little book.

I was given pocket money from the age of eight and could do whatever I chose with it. Some was spent and some was saved.

My childhood was blissful. I loved school, had lots of friends who adored coming over to my house. Mum welcomed everybody with open arms, butterfly cakes and blackcurrant squash.

I never wanted for much as a child, but I never had big treats. We didn't go on foreign holidays for example, but I was certainly treated at Christmas and birthdays with presents from my Father Christmas list. I had a strong notion of 'treats'. We'd have a KFC or fish and chips every Saturday as our 'treat day' and take an annual trip to Flambards Theme Park for a family day out.

Mostly our days out involved inexpensive activities such as a coastal walk to Cape Cornwall or Cot Valley or the beach. The best days of my life are the hundreds I've spent on Long Rock, Marazion, Sennen and Porthcurno beaches with nothing more than swim things, a towel and a homemade picnic.

A talent for numbers

My talent and love for maths was recognised early on in my life. My teachers embraced my love for maths and encouraged it. At the end of primary school, I was awarded a huge silver cup (that I got to keep) for being the most talented at mathematics. At the School Leavers Prize Giving day at the end of secondary school I again received the award for my mathematical ability.

Secondary school was a joy (well, most of the time!). At 11, I was in what I suppose you might call the middling clique: not the cool gang, the naughty gang or the loser gang. We were just normal girls, listening to Madonna, New Kids on the Block, Bros. We read Judy Blume and Virginia Andrews. We hung out at each other's houses every weekend, at Long Rock or Marazion beach whenever it was sunny. Being brought up in Penzance was pretty much the perfect childhood.

Age 15 I transferred to the cool gang: My soon-to-be best friend invited me on a night out to Chapel Street where (ironically?) the best pubs in Penzance were. From there I quickly became a member of the upper echelons of the cool gang. Weekends were all about working in Oliver's Shoe shop (age 14) or Dorothy Perkins (age 16), before heading home to get ready to go out. Evenings were spent in the many pubs of Penzance - the Admiral Benbow, the Regent, The Star - fake ID in hand, drinking snakebite and black until closing time, before stumbling on to the Zero, or Barn night clubs, dancing till dawn.

The end of childhood

Adult life hit me like a freight train in the summer of my 16th year. On June 26th I was awoken by my older sister to the news that my mum had died suddenly at the age of 58 of a heart attack. I was still a child, forced into adulthood too early.

My memories of the aftermath of mum's death are a blur. I remember the funeral. I remember my two best friends being there to support me, all of us numb with the realisation that we were still kids, yet one of us was suddenly without her mum. Those best friends' parents stepped in and scooped me up, having me over for tea, for sleep overs, doing the things that parents would do with their own children. I am forever grateful to them for the love they showed me.

My dad did not cope well. I had to take on my mum's role in running the house: I became the cook, the cleaner, the ironing girl. Each week my dad handed me an envelope filled with money to buy the weekly shopping. I clearly remember walking around Tesco with a shopping list and calculator. I was 16 and just about to start my A-Levels in Maths, Psychology and Business Studies. It was impossible not to think 'Surely this is a job that none of my 16-year-old friends are doing?' I found the unfairness of the situation galling every day of my late teenage years. I kept writing in my diary, 'Why me, what have I done to deserve this?' Counselling and therapy weren't so readily accessible in 1990s Cornwall.

At the supermarket I added up the prices of the food as I walked around the store, careful not go over my budget. I'd start at the freezer section, working my way from there to fruit and veg, bread, fridge area, groceries and finally treats. I always made sure I had enough left to get myself a treat at the end - some chocolate, cakes or crisps. I had control over the money, I could do whatever I wanted.

After a year of being the housekeeper my soon-to-be step-mum arrived and took over. I was so grateful to no longer have to do the housework. To this day I have an absolute hatred of house cleaning!

A-levels carried on. It was a challenging time. My grades were affected by my mum's death. My primary need was to escape. I felt university was what I was meant to do. The biggest belief my mum instilled in me was a sense of independence and freedom of choice: she gave me the confidence to know I could do anything I wanted in life, anything. If I wanted to change the world I could. She gave me freedom as a child to do whatever I wanted: when I made mistakes, I learnt from the consequences, developing a resilience through her faith in me that has remained with me throughout my life. It is almost as if she knew she was going to die, so imparted a sense of independence and ability to cope with life in me through those 16 years we had together.

I went off alone to visit all my university choices: Warwick, London, Manchester, Bristol, Exeter and Brighton. I chose Warwick and the best course in the country for maths, MORSE: maths, operational research, statistics and economics. My second choice was Brunel to study Maths, Statistics and Management.

Maths A-level was not, however, going well. I was predicted a B and I needed an A to get into Warwick. My dad ploughed money into this and paid for extra maths tutoring. It was not enough; I got the B for maths and my Warwick dreams were dashed. That fork of life happened and off I went to Brunel in West London for the next four years.

University and the Loss of Financial Control

At the end of my first year at university, five days before the year-end exams I got an early morning phone call on the pay phone in the corridor of our first-year flat. Cradling the receiver in my hand, I let out a scream. My dad had died of a heart attack the previous night. One of the lads from the ground floor flats came running out and wrapped his arms around me. My sister was leaving that minute to drive up to London from Penzance to collect me.

University was a wonderful time and an awful time. I lost control of my life. All my security was ripped away from me, including financial security and my life spiralled out of control. In the second year of university a good friend told me the truth, I was out of control and I needed to seek counselling. You need those outspoken friends in your life. I went straight to my personal tutor and counselling was arranged, my first experience with therapy.

University is where I learnt bad financial habits and began overspending. It's where I learnt how to play the system, how to maximise my grants and bursaries. I always worked in pubs, shops, plus a paid work placement for the third year of my degree. I learnt about the ease with which I could acquire credit cards, the 'free money' they granted me and the 'joy' of buying before I had earned/saved the money for my purchases. I took out the maximum loans and earned lots of money working. I spent every penny on music, clothes, nights out, travelling every weekend to see friends at other universities.

I got the best work placement job possible, with M&S on a business programme. The training was amazing as was the responsibility they gave me. I was running the Uxbridge store food department aged 21. The money was astounding. I carried on working for M&S throughout my fourth and final year, writing my dissertation for them via an IT project for the year 2000.

I graduated in 1999 with a 2:1 degree, with a first for my M&S dissertation. From there I sailed into a graduate job with HSBC in the city of London where I trained to become an accountant. My starting salary was £25k. I moved into a cottage in rural Kent with my much older boyfriend, commuting into London Bridge every day.

My 20s were an amazing time of fun, travel, working in great jobs with very little life responsibility. I passed all my accountancy exams, qualifying as an accountant with a few more letters after my name by the age of 24, Lynn Beattie BSc ACMA. I left HSBC and moved to Tesco a year later, moving from the Kent cottage into a three-bedroom house in Essex. I was now a homeowner with my boyfriend at the age of 25.

Growing up Financially

My financial education during my 20s came from my employers and working in finance, learning how to run a business in a financially sound way. I was surrounded by accountants and we would (happily and enthusiastically) talk money and personal finance. I learnt about the importance of saving, investments and a pension. At the same time, I was spending money like it was water. I don't have anything to show for my 20s in terms of investments beyond a bit of equity growth in a house. None of my investments or pensions date back to my 20s.

The relationship with the older man broke down in my late 20s; we became friends rather than lovers which made for an amicable split. I left with £25k, my share of the profit we made on the Essex house. I moved to Hertfordshire, much closer to my work with Tesco, where I was rising through the ranks quickly in their finance department. I was earning around £50k by then, making huge financial decisions for one of the biggest retailers in the world.

I moved on quickly relationship wise to one that would result in marriage, quickly learning another financial strategy: shouldering financial responsibility that wasn't directly mine.

Within three years, I was pregnant and married, 22 weeks pregnant on my wedding day to be precise. My 30s were spent trying to balance everything imperfectly perfectly. Dylan was born when I was 30, Josh at 32 and Jack at 35. After each maternity leave, I had to return to work sooner than I wanted, to pay the mortgage.

I moved companies each time, trying to find a way to make earning and being a mum work: first to T-Mobile (soon to merge with Orange and become EE) whose head office was a short drive away. I spent five years at EE, earning a lot by the time I left, around £80k a year. To this day I feel I don't have much financially to show for it. My divorce cost me a lot in both emotional strength and financial loss.

Towards Financial Freedom and Personal Transformation

I set up my money blogging website and company Mrs MummyPenny during my third maternity leave. I left EE to run Mrs MummyPenny full time in 2015. I left with a redundancy cheque, which gave me comfort that my bills were paid for around 18 months. It didn't quite work out, and we managed to stack up £16k of credit card debt during that time. Something that could be quite embarrassing for a money blogger who has built a reputation for guiding others on smart ways to manage their money.

However, as my mum taught me, I took ownership of my mistakes, working hard, following my own advice (living my truth…) and finally paying off the debt, in record time. I wrote about the experience believing, as I always have with Mrs MummyPenny, that maybe I can help others out there who are struggling with thorny issues like paying off debt.

Ironically, writing about how I managed to solely pay off that £16k debt in two years is one of the most successful stories I've told via my blog. The story has been picked up and retold in many major national publications and media including The FT, The Sun, Huffington Post, I Newspaper, BBC Radio and TV.

My marriage broke down and ended in 2019, and the divorce was granted in 2020. My new beginning and my transformation were complete.

Whilst I've always been good with numbers, as you can see from my story, that hasn't seamlessly translated to a life free from financial mistakes. Each chapter of my life, each 'mistake' I have made has brought with it lessons that have enabled me to figure out how to do things differently going forward. Like you, I've felt miserable and depressed at my financial situation at times, elated and free to spend (rather too) wildly at others. We are all, after all, human. It's not our mistakes that define us, it's what we do with them that counts.

There, in that murky water of having to pull ourselves out of life's swamps (whether of our own creation or not), having the ability to ask for help, to choose differently and to remain resilient, that is where the work of transformation truly happens.

I am now looking forward to financial freedom. I own my own house with some equity. I have no credit card debt; I have a decent pension and I have investments. And I have my wonderful business, which is priceless.

Chapter 2 – Our Money Memories

Our money beliefs are formed by the time we are seven years old according to a study from the University of Cambridge. Seven years old. This is why in this chapter we're going to look at our formative money memories, bringing light to a subject that I believe is rarely touched upon: How did we get to our current attitude towards money?

My Little Pony Stickers

My earliest memory of money is linked to my dad. He would collect coins in silver tankards that he kept in our feature piece wooden dresser where the china dining set, was kept, for best. The dining set that was only used for Christmas dinner. He would put every 20p and every 5p that he brought home in change from the daily newspaper and cigarette run (The Mirror for reference) in the tankards. I often did that paper and cigarette run for him to the bottom of my road. It was the early 80s and Penzance, much safer than now!

My job as a six-year-old was to count it for him every few months, bag it up and we'd take it to the bank together. I had full responsibility for the counting job. I also had an addiction to My Little Pony Panini stickers. I was desperate to complete the 600-strong collection. My mind whirred: Could I miscount the money, slip a few 20p's into my pocket and get an extra few packets of stickers?

So, I did. Every few days I would take a couple of 20p's and buy my stickers. I kept going until I completed that sticker collection. No one ever noticed.

My earliest money memory is simply that I could do whatever I wanted with money; it was easy to come by. I never felt guilty, sure I worried that I might be found out, but I never was.

Mum was a traditional housewife receiving weekly housekeeping from my dad, but she also went out to work to get extra money, for treats. I remember going on many cleaning jobs with her before I started school. She would clean local offices whilst I sat with books and dolls that I brought along for the adventure. I don't remember helping!

Despite my early sojourn into theft (!) my overall money upbringing was good in the early years. My dad's strong money saving ethos, combined with my mum's spirit to work hard for 'treat money' has continued throughout my life.

Fast forward to me as a 16-year-old girl

When my mum died everything changed. In addition to unspeakable grief I landed a huge lesson in managing finances, taking over that traditional housewifely role and, frankly, resenting it. Three years later, dad died, leaving me a homeless orphan.

Those two catastrophic events of my late teens flipped my money beliefs, leading to a life of hedonism, spending on material goods, and developing debts.

The good habits were always there in the background, but the bad beliefs and influences overloaded them, almost like the angel and the devil. Aged 40, having built a business on helping others to sort their finances out, I worked with the angelic side, addressing my debt, making and applying myself to a solid plan to get out of it.

Financial Education

I don't know about your financial education but schooled during the 80s and 90s there was little by way of 'life skills' on the curriculum in mine. Learning about cash flow forecasts during A-level business studies blew my mind! This was the first time anyone had handed me such a simple but enormously effective tool. A cash flow forecast asks you to write, month by month your income, list your various costs and see where you end up by the end of the year. See a simple example at the end of this chapter in the exercise section.

I remember wanting to get a job from as early an age as possible. I was desperate for my own cash for the freedom to buy whatever clothes I wanted and to save some money. Aged 14 I got a Saturday job at Oliver's Shoe Shop. My parents encouraged me, and I loved it. Setting up the shoe bins and racks in the morning and helping people with shoes all day long. I had some great managers who got me involved in the sales targets, cashing up the till and paperwork: they spotted my mathematical and financial talents and utilised them.

I learnt more about money management from my jobs than from my parents who never talked about money. I didn't know how much they earned, what the bills cost, if they were in debt or how much savings they had. The first I saw of income and bills was when I found one of my dad's payslips hidden in the paperwork cupboard. He earned £30k a year, I remember thinking, 'Wow that's good money,' and made a mental note to earn £30k as soon as I could.

I left for university aged 18, figuring out the whole process for myself. I applied for the place at university, the grant, sorted out accommodation, bank accounts, loans and overdrafts, by myself. I did everything, so I suppose I taught myself the basics of finance.

Regrettably, this included signing up to a credit card promising me free money: thank you Brunel branch of Barclays Bank. From the tender age of 18 I was introduced to the wonders of credit and the ability to buy things when I did not have the money saved to pay for them. I quickly progressed onto store cards as well and by the age of 20 I had store credit cards with Topshop, Miss Selfridges, Dorothy Perkins and Argos. And an addiction to buying stuff that I wanted, not needed. A credit card and debt problem that I fought with until the age of 42. More on that later.

There were positives from my self-taught finances. I always knew how to save money on everything I bought. Even if that was a 10% saving on my pile of clothes through opening a Topshop store card account. I was brilliant at getting marked down food. I was always in the bar for £1 a drink night.

More seriously, I knew how to get extra hardship grants from my university, and I worked from my second year through to the end of my fourth year to generate extra income. My fourth-year earnings were brilliant. I did a four-year sandwich degree and worked for Marks & Spencer in my third year, it was a great job, well paid as a management trainee, business placement scheme.

Again, I had brilliant management, whom I asked to carry on employing me in my fourth year if I did my dissertation as a project analysis study for M&S. They paid me something ridiculous (to a then 20-year-old) like £12 an hour to work in their IT systems department two days a week analysing, studying and writing about the cost/benefits of the Year 2000 (Year 2k bug) brand new till system for the whole M&S retail network. It was in Baker Street in London and I was able to get a free bus from their Stockley Park campus near to where I lived to work and back every day.

Ongoing Financial Education

I have spent much of my adult life learning more about the world of finances. I studied during my early 20s to become a CIMA management accountant and learnt invaluable skills about money management for a business that can be absolutely applied to personal finance.

I have engrossed myself in books, my favourites that I included in my website recommendations page. A standout book for me is 'It is Only Money and it Grows on Trees!' by Cara Macmillan. This is a wonderful guide explaining the concept of money and how it is viewed in different religions and societies. 'Feel the Fear and Do it Anyway' by Susan

Jeffers is a brilliant and accessible read. The first self-help book I ever read, it played to my risk-taking attitude.

I have embedded myself in the world of money, working in the finance departments of one of the biggest banks in the world, then with one of the biggest retailers, then with one of the biggest telecommunications companies. The people that I have worked with and the environment I have worked in has educated me hugely.

During my career I have attended some incredible courses that have aided my financial development, from leadership skills to women's development, to Gap negotiation skills training to name a few. All were incredible.

More recently, I've attended courses created by brilliant people who have equally embedded themselves in the subject of money, including one run by Emotionally Wealthy People. This was a life-changing course, picking apart - my money psychology and mindset and helping to rebuild it in a healthier way from a clearer understanding of my money needs, emotions, and beliefs.

Continuously learning, developing and transforming my approach to, and understanding of, money is of central importance to me and something I highly recommend. For all my financial education recommendations go to my recommendations page on my website. https://www.mrsmummypenny.co.uk/the-money-guide-to-transform-your-life-recommendations

Exercises for you to complete

Your financial education is important in how you manage money now, and your relationship with money. Understanding that is the first step in money management. Try to get under the skin of what you do and why you do it.

Practising these simple exercises will help you with this.

1.Think of your early money memories.

2.How did you manage money throughout your teens/20s/30s/40s/50s?

3.What was your parents' relationship with money like?

4.Are you a saver or a spender?

5.Have you always/ do you live beyond your means?

6.Do you live from one month to the next financially?

7.Do you like to surround yourself with lots of material things?

8.How important to you is your pension?

9.Do you own your own home?

10.Do you aim for financial freedom or independence?

A Cash Flow Forecast

A cash flow forecast requires you to write, month by month your income, list your various costs and see where you end up by the end of the year.

It is important to track cash over a period of time and create a cumulative total to ensure that you can ride the ups and downs of spending throughout the year.

In this worked example we can see that monthly costs are much higher in October to December in the run up to Christmas. But then lower in Feb/March (no council tax to pay). The cumulative total builds through to June but then starts to fall as costs get higher.

A Cash Flow Forecast example

	Income	Costs	+/-	Cumulative Total
January	2000	2000	0	
February	2000	1800	200	200
March	3000	1800	1200	1400
April	2000	2000	0	1400
May	2000	2200	-200	1200
June	3000	2000	1000	2200
July	2000	2200	-200	2000
August	2000	2200	-200	1800
September	2000	2000	0	1800
October	2000	2500	-500	1300
November	2000	2500	-500	800
December	2000	2500	-500	300

To download this document head to my book tools page on my website. https://www.mrsmummypenny.co.uk/the-money-guide-to-transform-your-life-tools

A Page for Your Chapter 2 Notes

Chapter 3 - Simple budgeting for Everyone

Let us (eat cake and) talk budgeting. Please do not scream out "boring", I will make it as painless and simple for you as I possibly can! Budgeting is at the core of getting in control of personal finance and understanding of your money. This is probably the simplest and most immediately effective way of transforming your finances.

Without changing anything about how or what you spend your money on, simply writing it all down (via a spending diary) will give you a sense of being back in the driving seat with your money.

Here is how I budget

I start with a detailed spending diary of everything that costs me any money. This will include monthly bills, PayPal payments, credit card payments, any cash transactions, any contactless payments, savings, pension contributions, business expenses. Absolutely everything.

I have found the best way to do this is to either write everything down at the end of each day in a crisp new spending diary notebook. Or to keep a list in a spreadsheet. I have tried both. Once in the habit (habits take six weeks to make or break!) you will go to that spending diary each day and write down your spending.

I enjoy the mental process of writing everything down and thinking about what I have spent and why. Was it an essential, was it an emotional purchase, was it worth the money spent or a waste?

Spending Diary

The inner workings of other people's finances aren't often on display and yet they can be very useful. During the Coronavirus Lockdown I published a weekly record of my spending that gave me such an insight into my spending, emotions, needs and wants. You can find all of these on my website in the Monday Money section.

One of the most powerful ways of using a spending diary is to spot emotionally 'down' days and see what happens to your spending on those days. I know I have a tendency towards emotional spending, sometimes it makes me feel better, but does it? Do I really feel better after that initial buzz of buying something new that I probably already have another three versions of at home? I counted my blouses recently. I have 22. This is excessive, I must stop buying blouses.

I have shown an example from week nine of my Coronavirus Lockdown spending diaries.

I tended to spend around £400 per week and this week was no exception at £426. There are a couple of examples of my emotional spending creeping through into here. £70 was spent on the build of a customised skateboard for one of my children who was going through a tough time. I landed a huge Mrs MummyPenny contract and celebrated with a bottle of champagne for £45. On reflection both spends could have been avoided. But also, I could afford them at the time, life is not all about restriction with spending, it is also about treating yourself.

Date	£	Detail
18/05/2020	19.17	Co-op
19/05/2020	3.50	Simmonds bakery
19/05/2020	14.00	Harry's Razor blades
19/05/2020	27.12	B&M cleaning stuff and bits
19/05/2020	70.00	Skateboard customisation
20/05/2020	37.50	Cleaner
20/05/2020	62.81	Vets Tick removal
21/05/2020	7.99	Book Amazon
21/05/2020	12.99	Basketball Amazon
22/05/2020	21.54	LCN domain renewal business expense
22/05/2020	21.50	Co-op
22/05/2020	27.00	KFC Friday night takeaway
23/05/2020	45.17	Off License champange, drinks
24/05/2020	10.00	Will annual charge
24/05/2020	0.99	Drive film Amazon
24/05/2020	5.40	Off license
24/05/2020	20.00	Bakery items farmers market
24/05/2020	9.65	Fruit and Veg
24/05/2020	10.50	Hype shoes Jack
Total	426.83	

Exercises to Complete

Create your own spending diary

Firstly, I suggest you follow the spending diary example in the previous section. Once you have done this exercise for a month, you're ready to create your first budget.

You can download my Excel spending diary template from my website, head to my book tools page on my website. https://www.mrsmummypenny.co.uk/the-money-guide-to-transform-your-life-tools

It is ever so simple, you just add the date, amount and what the spend was. Then categorise into different spending types, groceries, petrol, essential bills, household expenses, family entertainment, school costs, childcare etc. Take a look and have a go yourself.

At the end of each day, week or month, you can add up your spends and see in reality and with mindfulness what you are spending money on.

Create your own budget

You can download my budget tool from my website, head to my book tools page on my website. https://www.mrsmum-mypenny.co.uk/the-money-guide-to-transform-your-life-tools

Very simply put, a budget compares your income and your expenses. The first key test of any budget is - Is my income higher than my expenses? For most of my life as an example, my expenses were higher than my income, hence having debt for most of my adult life.

Income

When you are employed your income is relatively simple with an amount that tends to stay the same each month. This is whole different situation if you work varying overtime hours, are on a zero hours contract, have several jobs or are self-employed.

Speaking from personal experience as a self-employed person, I use my base line income here, a number that I know my income will never fall beneath (or has never fallen beneath for the past two years). Or you could use your average monthly income over the past, say, six months and use that as your income in your budget.

Don't forget to include income from things like Facebook/eBay sales and income from any benefits you receive.

Use your spending diary to create a list of your expenses.

Start with your essential, must-pay bills: I include rent, mortgage, child maintenance payments, council tax, electricity/gas, water, school costs, broadband, mobile, insurance (life, car, pet, home, income protection – I will talk more about insurance later in Chapter 11), loan payments, credit card payment, car finance, car tax, personal tax and national insurance if self-employed.

Next, list your regular variable monthly living costs, including groceries, petrol, train travel, eating out, takeaways, clothes, family entertainment, personal fun money, gifts, charity donations.

The next thing to list out is more irregular costs that might hit every two months, every six months. Things like annual insurance policies, vets, dentist, contact lenses, haircuts, children's birthdays, Christmas, school trips, car servicing, Work out how much these would cost over a year and then divide this number by 12 to get a monthly allocation.

And then list out positive movements of cash into savings for the future you, be that immediate future or further into the future when you would like to be financially free (or not working!). Include here emergency savings, holiday savings, investments, children's savings, pension contributions and mortgage overpayments.

Then you start adding in your numbers that you can transfer over from your spending diary. I have created a simple budget tool that you can download from my website No need for you to recreate yourself when you can use my simple model. The spreadsheet will add up everything for you and give you a balance at the bottom of your income (money in) less your expenses (money out).

You can download my budget tool from my website, head to my book tools page on my website. https://www.mrsmummypenny.co.uk/the-money-guide-to-transform-your-life-tools

How scary was that? I know it is maybe an hour or two of work, but well worth the time and the effort. Let us talk about the number at the bottom of your budget. Do your expenses exceed your income? If so, then the next chapter is for you.

A Page for Your Chapter 3 Notes

Chapter 4 – Debt – The Scariest Four-Letter Word in the English Language?

Debt is probably one of the biggest taboos out there financially speaking. It's also one of the biggest causes of stress and anxiety. We live in a society that at times seems to both frown on debt whilst simultaneously handing it out as though it were sweeties, to be indulged in and enjoyed.

There's an awful lot of moral shaming attached to debt. In some senses we're made to feel as though we've failed to behave 'properly' by getting into debt: the negatives truly come out when it comes to our inability to repay it. Debt can feel like a heavy monster hung round our necks, despite setting out with the best of intentions when we signed on the dotted line for the cash in the first place.

Freeing yourself from that financial bind though – oh my gosh, now that *is* an empowering feeling, and one I'd love for you to experience.

My Debt Story

I have spent most of my adult life in debt. Be that credit cards, loans, money owed to friends. I have felt that shame and embarrassment, that I was out of control with my money. The shame that I was unable to repay that debt in good time, despite having a great job. It became a belief that it was okay to be in debt if it was on 0% credit cards. NO!! That money was not mine: I was borrowing from my future self.

I have a well-publicised experience of being in £16k of debt and paying it back in two years. I shared the story in the FT and The Sun in June 2019, how it happened and how I paid it back. I wanted to reach a huge audience to inspire others to do the same.

Sharing my story felt scary and made me feel vulnerable: by the age of 40 I was a well-known personal finance blogger, and I 'should have known better'. Practise what you preach is a phrase drummed into me from a young age. But coming clean, sharing my story with my readers to reveal everything, the emotions, the helplessness, the support from friends, the failings, the slippery slope of going backwards, the mum guilt, the lack of support from a partner, was ultimately hugely healing – for me and as I discovered for many of the people reading the piece.

My debt history

I first learnt about debt working in Dorothy Perkins where, as a 16-year-old, I happily sold store cards to my customers, getting them to tick the payment protection box. We, the staff, were incentivised to sell store cards and got extra points for the payment protection insurance- PPI (an insurance on your purchases, now deemed irresponsibly sold by financial companies, with huge refunded given). I would get a £1 gift voucher for selling a store card, bumped up to £2.50 if the customer ticked payment protection. 'It will only cost you £1.75 for every £100 you spend' - I can even remember my sales patter; everyone ticked the box.

I bought into the myth that credit and store cards were free money. It certainly felt as though it was, as you got a 10% discount on your first purchase!

Arriving at university at the age of 18 I was handed my first credit card by my bank. This was the beginning of more than two decades' worth of addiction to debt and of having to teach myself how to escape its clutches.

It was a slippery slope that saw me teeter on the edge of debt ruin several times in my life. There were points when I wasn't sure if I could pay the mortgage the following month, but still had a £300 minimum debt repayment to make. By my late 20s I was working for Tesco in their head office as a commercial manager. It was a great job, but I was living beyond my means using credit cards to buy things I wanted (not needed) before I could even afford them. Every bonus I received went straight into debt repayment.

Eventually I reached a huge debt low. I decided to extend our house after recently having a third baby boy. Why did I decide this? There was an element of not wanting to move to a new house, due to the expense of buying a new house. And there was an element of keeping up with my friends, in wanting a bigger house.

The extension budget rapidly went out of the window. I had originally budgeted to spend £60k but the final spends came in at £70k. The extension building bit was around £40k, funded from an additional mortgage loan. But the remaining £30k spend was an entire house of new windows, new carpets, new sofa, dining table, the whole house redecorated, landscaped garden, driveway paved. I could go on. Much of this was nice to have, not essential. The spending snowballed, and before I knew it I was buying new everything and no one was stopping me, I was out of control on a mad spending spree and ignoring the growing balance on the spreadsheet of spending that I was keeping. The extra £30k was money I did not have. Another £20k mortgage loan was taken out and £10k added to my existing credit card debt, taking my total credit card debt at the time to £20k. All in my name.

I had no way of paying back £20k of credit cards. I started to worry about when the 0% interest periods ended, and the debt started to increase with 18-20% interest charges. A strange thing then happened. As I mentioned in Chapter 1 my dad died when I was 19 and his wife, my then stepmother had inherited all my parents' money. Soon after my debt crisis moment my stepmother sent me an unexpected cheque for £17k in the post. WOW!

That £17k late inheritance went straight into mostly paying off that house extension credit card overhang. I am pretty sure I went on a treat spending binge with some of it and around £8k of debt remained on a 0% deal which felt more manageable.

The Debt Trap

I had to return to work full time to a high earning job after my third child was born to pay the now large monthly mortgage and the debt repayments. My salary was necessary to pay for the lifestyle I had created. By then, I had launched Mrs MummyPenny, but there was no way I could follow my dream as I felt trapped by the cost of the lifestyle I had created.

Four years later I had long left the safety of my employed job after taking the huge leap into self-employment. I was sick of not seeing my children, having bosses trying to control me, all for a salary maintaining a lifestyle that was too expensive. I needed to break free!

I had previously taken redundancy from EE, and used that money to pay for life, bills, food and holidays whilst I built up my business without having to worry too much about it generating income.

By the time two years had passed between leaving EE and working full time on Mrs MummyPenny I had spent my £40k redundancy and had a credit card debt balance of a large amount. I remember ignoring it for six months. I knew the balance was rising and starting to get out of control, but I needed to buy food, pay the mortgage etc. Grocery shopping, school dinners, boys' clothes, all went onto the credit card. My business income was on the rise, my average turnover was around £2k per month. This was now just enough to cover my share of the monthly bills, but not enough to start paying back big chunks of debt; I was on minimum repayment mode.

A couple of years later, straight after my 40th birthday blowout holiday to Las Vegas (that I totally could not afford, which also went on credit cards), I added the debt up. £16k. Oh my gosh. I worked out it would take me six and a half years to repay the debt based on my minimum monthly payments. This felt depressing, hopeless, never-ending.

I needed a plan. I set my mind to it and paid off that minimum monthly payment and paid more when I could afford it, when I earned more, and when I saved extra each month. By April 2019, the £16k was paid off in full.

It's important to pay more when you can afford it, it will help you to clear the debt quicker. The satisfaction I felt of paying off a £500 chunk of debt was good! Getting me closer to that debt free position.

Over to you/Exercises

Here are the steps I took to pay off my credit card debt. My steps differ to other well published methods, but I feel like they kept me motivated and clear on my final goal. It is a method using logic and I prioritised my mental health with these steps.

If you're feeling out of control and are not ready to make a plan yourself, please, please go straight to the Citizens Advice (CAB), Christians Against Poverty or Step Change. Three amazing and FREE places for debt advice. For all links and recommendations in this book, head to my recommendations page on my website. https://www.mrsmummypenny.co.uk/the-money-guide-to-transform-your-life-recommendations

Step 1 – Face Up to your Debt. Write it down.

You have already taken the first step by recognising you have a problem and are reading this section of my book, congratulations! Now is the time to get the credit card and loan details of everything you owe. Call the companies for an up-to-date balance, interest rate and minimum repayment.

Write it all down and face that reality of how much you have in debt. It might be £1,000, £10,000 or £50,000. You need to face up to the reality of that debt. It is not your money, it belongs to Barclaycard, MBNA, Virgin Money or whoever your cards/loans are with. It needs to be paid back.

Step 2 – Get rid of the Cards. Cut them up/freeze them.

Obviously record the important information, card numbers and contact numbers. And then destroy the cards. Do not spend on them again. You do not want these cards to go up in balance through extra spending. You could freeze them in a block of ice if you cannot bear to destroy them. But once they are gone, you cannot spend on them.

Step 3 – Come up with a plan

Well done for steps 1 and 2. They are tough. Now you must come up with a plan. You can do this by yourself, but it will help you immensely if you can talk it through with someone else, particularly someone who will not judge and who is good with money.

Work out some basics. For each debt, what is the balance, what is the minimum monthly payment and what is the interest rate. If interest free, for how long?

For example, when I faced the problem head on I worked out the following:

- I had £7,500 on a Barclaycard; interest free for another three months
- £1,000 on a 'holiday money' Halifax card. Interest rate of 18%
- £1,500 on a Barclays Business card. Interest rate of 19%
- £5,500 on a Virgin Credit Card. Interest free for a further 18 months
- Total of £15,500 but let's round it to £16k for simplicity

My total minimum payments were £200 per month, that I could afford to pay.

Step 4 – Restructure any debt if you can

My priority was to find a longer interest-free deal on a new credit card to move that Barclaycard balance that was just about to become interest chargeable. I found a deal with MBNA, interest free for 42 months. With a hefty three percent transfer fee of £225. But it would give me breathing space and I would not be paying the standard rate of 18/19% in three months' time.

Do this if you have a credit rating that allows you, many decent credit card companies will let you check your eligibility by carrying out a soft credit check on you. A soft check won't affect your credit rating, but a hard check, the final check to ensure you can repay the debt, will. Several hard checks on your credit file will affect your credit rating.

You can check your credit rating for free with the agencies including Credit Karma, Experian and Equifax. Your credit score and record are very important to any application for credit, its worthwhile checking it every few months. I personally have a free e-mail alert set up when anything changes via Credit Karma.

Step 5 – Start to pay off the debt that is costing you money in interest FIRST

Clear the most expensive debt with the highest interest first! This is the debt that is costing you money every month with a 10-20-30% APR (annual percentage rate). This interest charge can cost hundreds each month, clear the highest rate debt first.

In my case the Barclays Business and Halifax were cleared within a couple of months. They both had 18/19% interest being added to the balances.
After the interest-charging cards were cleared, I was left with two large balances on 0% cards. This is when you work on the card with the smallest balance first. I worked on clearing the Virgin card first with a balance of £5,500, it was also the shorter interest-free period. The aim here being a mindset challenge to clear the balance and have the mental satisfaction that it has been cleared. Keep your minimum payments the same though, despite having cleared cards, just move that money you were paying each month to the next debt.

I set a monthly minimum payment at what I knew I could afford; £200 per month was being paid off the Virgin card and the MBNA card was set at min payment, starting at £80, although this reduced as my balance reduced. You might be better off setting a fixed minimum repayment.

Every month this minimum would be paid along with anything else I could afford. Some months this was the basic £280 per month, but other months I was able to pay more towards the debt. Even if it was an extra £50 it was worth paying it towards the debt and getting closer to being debt free.

Do everything you can to save money and make extra money, more on this in chapter 6.

Step 6 – At the same time, build up an emergency fund

This is an essential piece of guidance. At the same time as paying off your credit card you should also be putting money into an emergency fund. This is an easy to access pot of money for emergencies, such as car repairs, a boiler needing repairs or a new washing machine. It is NOT for holidays, clothes and things that you want, rather than need.

For every extra £100 I was paying into my debt I was also putting £100 into my emergency fund. This gave me a huge peace of mind that if I did need money then I could dip into this to pay for that emergency if needed.

I kept doing this until my emergency fund got to an amount that I was comfortable with. I recommend that your emergency fund is between three and six months of your essential expenses, more on emergency funds in chapter 5.

Step 7 – Keep going until the debt is gone

It might take you two years, or it might take you five, but keep going. Keep making those monthly payments until the debt is gone and you are free. Expect ups and downs. Expect to feel like the journey may never end, but you will get some glimmers of hope and the light at the end of the tunnel does get brighter. And then suddenly you reach the day when you are debt free.

I slipped, a couple of times. The summer holiday always gets me, higher living expenses and lower income. You may well slip, but please do not beat yourself up too much. Every day, week, month is a new day, week, month, and you can re-set positive intentions to get that debt to zero.

I shared my story on Instagram and on my blog throughout the two years, just head to my blog and go to the debt section to read more. The Instagram community was incredibly helpful during my debt repayment, offering motivation and congratulations at every step. You could set up an anonymous account to do this as a great motivational technique. Great hashtags to search for are #debtfree #debtfreecommunity #debtfreejourney

Step 8 – Love and Gratitude

During your debt repayment and afterwards, send out love and gratitude to every person who supports you in your journey, who sends you a message or a comment. These people will get you through it. One day they might need your support and you can repay the favour.

I receive so many messages from people, like me, like you, reading this book who have decided to face that debt journey, having been inspired by my story. These honestly make my job the best there ever is. Making a difference to people's lives is hugely motivational and inspiring to me to carry on doing what I am doing. Keep sending those messages, they make my day a happier day.

A Page for Your Chapter 4 Notes

Chapter 5 - The Emergency Savings Fund

The emergency fund (also known as the f*ck-off fund) is the most important savings pot to prioritise before you start looking at any other kind of savings. In my 20s I was in a relationship that I needed to leave, but I didn't have the savings in place to do this. I lived with a man with whom I had a joint mortgage, it was financially reasonably complex, though no children or marriage, thank goodness.

I decided the relationship was over, but then, before leaving I spent six months building up my f*ck-off fund. I had a good job, so I stopped spending and started stashing away as much cash as possible. Once I felt financially comfortable, I had the conversation about feeling the relationship was over. He wasn't surprised, and I moved out the same day. It was all very amicable. Two months later he transferred me 50% of the equity gain from the house. The relationship ended with two happy individuals.

My emergency fund gave me the freedom to walk away from a relationship that I did not want. Many years later I followed a similar approach with my divorce, ensuring that my credit card debt was repaid and that my emergency fund was securely in place.

I can only imagine how awful it must feel to be trapped in a relationship because of financial reasons. An emergency fund will help you to get out.

Purpose of the Emergency Fund

The emergency fund does what it says on the tin. It is there for unexpected emergencies. Maybe the car needs four new tyres, or the washing machine has broken down or the boiler has stopped working. Or even something bigger like a redundancy for you, or maybe your partner. My emergencies this year alone have included the vacuum cleaner dying, a roof tile being blown off in a storm and the kitchen tap leaking incessantly and needing replacing.

The emergency fund is also there to protect you if you have a sudden loss of income. What would you do if you were made redundant and could not find another job? What would you do if you became seriously ill, too ill to work? What would you do if an unprecedented virus hits the globe and your income reduces by 20%? What would you do if your partner suddenly leaves you?

There are so many circumstances that the emergency fund can be used for. If you have it there as a safety net it helps you feel safe and reassured that if the worst does happen, and inevitably it does, then you have the next three to six months covered.

Paying off debt and building an Emergency Fund

I will always recommend anyone paying off debt to build an emergency fund at the same time. Exactly what I did when I was paying off my £16k debt in two years. Every month I would pay off at least £280 of minimum payments and put some money into my emergency savings also. I kept going until I had three months' worth of essential expenses stashed away in my emergency savings.

This made me feel safe and reassured that if I needed some emergency money I had it there in savings, rather than having to go back into debt. After paying for those inevitable emergencies I would always work to get my emergency fund back up to the level it was at.

When the Debt is Repaid

Once your debt is cleared it's time to focus on building that strong emergency fund, up to a recommended six months' worth of money. I recommend also that you keep it in a separate saving account with a different bank. Use the best buy tables in the weekend newspaper or online for the best instant access bank account. This is key for your emergency fund; it must be held in an instant access account where you have immediate access to your money. I can get my money transferred to my bank account within seconds.

Short Term Savings Accounts

As well as emergency fund I like to have some other savings pots. Pots for things that are important for me to have for my mental wellbeing, i.e. holidays. And I like to have a few of them a year, a summer holiday with my boys, another one with my friends and then a few long weekends throughout the year. A holiday savings fund is an important one for me to have.

Most modern challenger banks now offer the saving pot system, banks such as Starling and Monzo. I have a main bank account balance and then I have various pots where I can allocate money to. The money disappears from my main bank account balance so it FEELS like I can't spend it, in reality it is sitting in my savings pots that I have renamed to things I am saving for in the short term. These pots can include spends like; - holiday fund, annual car repairs/insurance/tax, income tax, Christmas costs, family birthday costs.

A Page for Your Chapter 5 Notes

Chapter 6 - Money Saving Ideas

It's easy to look at a budget, a debt repayment plan or a savings goal and feel a bit helpless. Where on earth are you going to get the money to balance the budget more successfully, pay off your debt and get those savings pots sorted?

This is where employing some clever money savings schemes can really help. In this chapter I share with you some of the ways in which you can shave pounds off your spending – pounds that can be redeployed in other areas of your life, helping you to become debt free and in a position to spend on the basis of what you've saved rather than having to borrow, again, against the future.

My money saving expertise

Something that I have consistently been is an expert at money saving on everything. Sure, I have spent a lot of money, but I have always saved whilst doing this. I always get the best deal for monthly expenses and regular spends.

Since a young age I was the go person for the best savings account, or the best mortgage deal. Before Mrs MummyPenny was created, I would help people with energy switching recommendations or I would help people to go through all their bills and/or debts and work out many ways to save.

It was a natural step to turn my life passion into my business.

A huge part of paying down debt or creating a positive gap between your income and expenses bigger is to save money on your household bills and regular spends. And by this point you will have done your budget using my Excel spreadsheet and will know clearly how much you are spending each month and on what.

I will talk you through each type of expense and explain how to save money and get the best deal. The brands I mention and detail in my recommendations section are brands that I personally use and put my money where my mouth is! I will also let you know if I get a refer a friend fee, and if there is a bonus for you too!

I closely check the brands I work with, I check their ethics match mine, that they excel at looking after their staff, thus consequently providing brilliant customer service, (one leads to the other). I check the companies are financially viable and that they have the best environmental policies.

This is the process that I go through with my budget

Essential bills – A quick review of you Direct Debits

Before going into the detail of the essential bills saving ideas you must go through your direct debits and work what is essential. Do you really need to pay for Sky TV, Netflix and Amazon Prime? Do you really need the expensive boiler insurance or the oven insurance? Question everything and cancel it if it feels like an unnecessary expense.

I go through my direct debits every six months and do a quick review to check that they are all essential and still needed. I have gotten rid of things like dishwasher insurance (if it does break, the money comes from my emergency fund), mobile phone insurance, magazine subscriptions and monthly contact lenses. Likewise, I do the same with my business, where I have so many monthly subscriptions: do I really need professional Zoom, Microsoft Office, accounting software, podcast hosting. Currently yes, I do, but it's worth having a good look through all your direct debits. If you feel it is unnecessary, go online or call them up and cancel it. An immediate significant money saving can be made there.

Review the Essential Monthly Costs

Mortgage or Rent

Most likely this is your biggest bill that must be paid each month. Oh, to be mortgage free (I say with a long mortgage term remaining). There are often ways to cut costs here. I re-mortgaged to buy out my ex-husband as part of our divorce settlement. I got a 1.39% mortgage rate! At the time of writing (June 2020) mortgage rate are at an all-time low, and likely will stay this way for a while.

Talk to an independent mortgage broker who can assess the entire market for the most appropriate fixed or variable rate mortgage with fees to work out how much money per month you could save. My recommendation for a mortgage broker can be found on my website https://www.mrsmummypenny.co.uk/the-money-guide-to-transform-your-life-recommendations

If you can move to a new mortgage deal with a lower interest rate, then you will save a huge chunk of monthly expenses.

A fixed rate mortgage gives you the stability of an agreed interest rate and the same monthly payment for a period of time. A variable rate mortgage moves with the Bank of England Base Rate and your monthly payments will do the same.

You can have a repayment or interest only mortgage. The repayment mortgage means that you are paying off the loan balance as well as the interest. At the end of your total mortgage term your house will be fully paid off and owned fully. An interest only mortgage means that you are only paying the interest payments, and not towards the actual cost of the house. An interest only mortgage can be a short-term fix, as monthly payments are lower, but I would not recommend for the long term.

A worked example

If you have a mortgage of £200k outstanding on a 25-year term, with a fixed rate of 2.49% your monthly repayments (repayment basis, not interest only) will be £896 per month.

Switch this to say 1.49% on a two-year fixed deal and your monthly mortgage payment goes down to £799. A saving of nearly £100, and this is pure interest you are saving. Your monthly repayment will still reduce your mortgage balance in the same. Use the mortgage calculator as mentioned on my website recommendations page to play around with your own numbers.

Rent Savings

A bit trickier, this one. If you have a good relationship with your landlord or letting agency be sure to negotiate your rent when you start living somewhere or when your rent is up for renewal. Rent absolutely can be negotiated down. The monthly charge is never set in stone.

Council Tax

This is the tax that pays for the police, fire service, refuse collection, local county council and parish council. It is a usually a large bill. It depends on the value of your house as it stood in 1990. Be sure to check that your house is classified using the correct rates band. I live in a four-bed semi-detached house in Hertfordshire, Band D and my council tax is around £190 per month, paid over 10 months. Check out your local council website for more information on your council tax.

As I am a newly single mum, I applied immediately for a single person discount of 25%, my new council tax is £150. Still a large bill, but at least lower. I like to pay it over ten months, that way I get two months March and April-when I do not have to pay my council tax; this feels like a nice bonus that I put towards debt repayment or maybe towards something fun like a holiday.

Utilities – Electricity, Gas

These are usually also large bills, often way more than £100 per month. It is easy to save money here though by simply doing an energy comparison and switching to a company with cheaper energy rates. Let's be honest here about energy. It's all the same, whichever company that you pay your money to. The only things that differ are the cost and the levels of customer service (and bizarrely, paying more doesn't guarantee better customer service in my experience!).

My recommendation for Octopus Energy, the company that I use can be found on my website https://www.mrsmummypenny.co.uk/the-money-guide-to-transform-your-life-recommendations.

Get a Smart Meter

Smart meters are being rolled out across the UK for the accurate measurement of electricity and gas use. Your energy company will fit one for free. My smart meter gives me real time energy usage information and I know that my monthly usage bills are 100% accurate. No more estimates of bills and manual meter reading.

Plus, now I know exactly how much energy things are using in my home I have changed my behaviour. Everything is switched off at the wall, I nag everyone about switching off lights, I rarely use my tumble dryer and use my slow cooker more often than the cooker. I fill the kettle with enough water for that one cup and use the economy settings on my washing machine and dishwasher.

During the winter I compared a day of heating on during the day to heating off during the day. With the heating on my energy cost £3.50 and without the heating cost £2.50. If we did this every day this is a saving of £30 a month (it would be very cold though!).

If you are getting a smart meter fitted, do check that is a second-generation meter to ensure that the meter still works when switching from one supplier to another.

Water Bill

Your water bill is more set in stone: you must pay the company that services your area and you cannot switch. However, you can choose to be on a water meter if you move to a property that is on water rates. The general guidance is if you have fewer people than bedrooms it is most likely cheaper to have a water meter. Just call up your water company and they will sort it for you for free.

Broadband

I have no loyalty to any broadband provider and tend to switch every year to get the best deal. With broadband you have two choices BT (or the many companies that use the BT cables, PlusNet, TalkTalk, EE etc) or Virgin who use a different cable system.

You can get amazing cashback deals on broadband with the companies desperate to get you on board as customer who then hope that you stay beyond the length of your 12-18-month contract. Check that the monthly cost is competitive, and that the cashback is a good deal.

An example is me changing from TalkTalk to Virgin. I needed fast great quality broadband as I work from home and have lots of devices being used with three boys. I got £120 cashback moving over to Virgin on a £38 a month 12-month contract. The cash back took it down to £28 per month. One year later I have moved from Virgin to EE, my new 18-month contract is £24 per month and I received £100 cash back. Taking my monthly cost down to £18.44. A saving of nearly £10 per month.

TopCashback is my cashback company of choice they often offer higher rates of cash back compared to others. I have had an account for seven years and my total cash back earned is at £3,500 (yes you read that correctly £3,500) that I have earned in cashback discounts and refer a friend payments.

Everything I buy online I push through TopCashback to get an extra discount. Simply put, you open an account and search for a retailer on TopCashback first. They are all on there! Once you find, say Nike, click on the box that whizzes you through to Nike to make your purchase. You will then be credited with a cash back amount, this is currently 4% of the purchase total for Nike (April 2020). Mental note, DJ, my eldest does need new trainers!

Mobile Phone

There is always a better deal to had with your mobile phone when you come to end of your contract. I have recently moved to a Sim only plan saving myself a huge £32 per month!

I would also recommend negotiating a deal, having worked in the mobile phone industry, I know you can walk into a shop, or phone their call centre to get yourself a deal that is better than what they often have advertised on their website or window poster. Particularly if you are an existing customer, they will want to keep you with a good deal.

Traditional mobile phone contracts last 24 month and include the phone, normally for free as a sweetener. The contract costs you maybe £40 a month for two years meaning you are paying £960 for a phone that maybe cost the phone company £4-500 (I used to work for EE!).

To save money look into buying the phone separately and taking a Sim Only contract covering just data, calls and texts. If you already have a phone that is out of contract and it still works then just pay for the Sim only contract. It's also an idea to look at the data on your contract, do you really need 20 GB of data when you are often at home with Wi-Fi? Reducing your data on your contract can save you money too.

To get a truly independent view on a mobile phone deal is difficult as many of the comparison sites are skewed towards those companies who pay them more money to move their deals to the top of their recommended list. Uswitch is the best comparison company for both mobile and broadband, just beware of my warnings, this is how most comparison sites work, sadly.

TV Package

Many of us pay for expensive TV packages. Personally, I have a TV licence, Netflix and Amazon Prime (begrudgingly paid the £79 annual fee in one go to get my music, books, tv and film and free postage and packaging). I spend £22.19 per month on TV. You may also have Sky TV, Virgin TV, BT Sports, Heyu, Now TV, Apple TV, Disney+, the list goes on and on as more new companies enter the market.

My question to you is to check that you need every TV package. If you have Netflix do you need Amazon Prime TV, Sky and Disney+ as well? It's a debate that I often have with myself, so am limiting myself to just Netflix and Amazon Prime. I often find great stuff to watch on iPlayer and More 4 anyway which is on Freeview and covered by your TV licence. Anything you deem you don't watch enough of, cancel. You can always switch it back on if you miss it too much.

Make a call to Sky, Virgin or BT the main companies that host your TV, Broadband and landline in one package and see what they can do to reduce your monthly cost. If you are out of contract, they will always offer you a better deal. But you need to be proactive here, call them. Go to the customer retention team, who are specifically there to keep you as customer. A better deal and a saving are there for your taking.

You can also avoid paying for your TV licence if you never watch live BBC TV and do not watch iPlayer.

Insurance

There are many insurances that are important to have. I have listed four here but there are many more that you might have. Firstly, you should assess how important the insurance is to you. For example, I used to have dishwasher insurance, but paid £18 a month for a year and never made a claim. That was £216 I spent on insurance; I could have bought a whole new dishwasher with that. I cancelled it after a year and saved myself £18 a month!

All insurance should be compared and checked every year, never let a policy auto-renew unless you want to be stung with a high renewal charge. You can check your insurance policies on comparison websites, my favourites listed on my recommendations page.

I recommend honesty in all insurance applications, as you risk not being accepted for pay outs if you tell porkies to reduce an insurance price.

Home Insurance

Home insurance is normally as essential requirement when you have a mortgage. And it is an important insurance to cover you for loss and damage to your home and contents.

You have buildings and contents insurance. Building insurance covers you for damage to the house from fire, storm and covers you for the house to rebuilt. Content insurance insured the things inside. Be sure to get cover that is enough for your contents, you might be surprised how much it would cost to replace everything in your home if there was a fire for example.

Your contents insurance can be standard or have accidental cover added. Handy when your toddler throws something at the TV screen and break it (this has happened twice to me).

Car Insurance

Car Insurance is the law! You have to have it. There is fully comprehensive and third, party, fire and theft. I would only have fully comprehensive to cover me for everything and I protect my no claims bonus that is now at its maximum.

My car insurance is checked every year based on comparison site checks. Car insurance is my least favourite bill to investigate value for money. I hate doing it, but it must be done. My renewal quote sent through in March 2020 was £480. I ran a comparison using the TopCashback comparison site and got my quote down to £420 (ensuring that I was using a reputable insurance firm that I had heard of with good real customer Trustpilot scores).

£420 still felt like a lot, especially as I only paid £280 the previous year. The only difference this year was it was one adult on the policy, after removing a second driver, plus one speeding ticket. Both changes have made my car insurance much more expensive.

There are many ways to save with car insurance;- parking the car in a garage, having a car security, driving less miles, having a higher excess are some way to save.

I decided to try out a different car insurance product, something new, a pay-as-you-go car insurance company, savings hundred, all the details are in my recommendations page on my website. https://www.mrsmummypenny.co.uk/the-money-guide-to-transform-your-life-recommendations.

Travel Insurance

Not an essential insurance, but it's something that I ever travel without. I have annual travel insurance for myself and my children, it works out much cheaper to buy in one annual amount.

Travel insurance is an important one, to be taken out the day you book your holiday, not just before you go! It will cover you for illness on holiday, delays and compensation, theft or loss of belongings whilst broad, repatriation, many rare occurrences. But for the sake of around £50-60 per year for an annual travel insurance policy, it is worth having. You can buy individual trip insurance, compare the prices of both to see which is better value depending on how many times you travel in a year.

If you choose to purchase travel insurance annually, as with any other insurance you take out always compare and most likely switch companies every year for insurance deal. All details in my recommendations page on my website.

Pet Insurance

Again, not an essential insurance and something that many people with pets don't have. Hands up, I have a cat, Trev, and he isn't insured. If I had a dog I would pay for insurance, I have heard too many horror stories from friends about huge vet bills.

To compare pet insurance providers check my recommendations page on my website.

Insurance (Life, Health, Income Protection, Critical Illness)

I have a whole chapter 11 on these types of insurance later in the book. I believe they are essential products nearly everybody should have, particularly if you have dependants and a mortgage.

Very simply put, life insurance pays out if you die, normally a fixed amount that at least covers your mortgage. Health insurance is a policy to cover any health needs you have, particularly useful to skip the NHS waiting lists and get non-emergency treatments quicker.

Income protection insurance will cover your monthly income if you lose your income due to illness. Critical illness insurance will pay out a lump sum if you are diagnosed with a life-threatening condition.

Reviewing Other spends

As part of the budgeting process discussed in Chapter 3 you will have kept a spending diary, so you now know what else you spend money on each month. I will try to go through these in priority and spend order.

Groceries

I have referenced my real-life spending diary with full details on what I spent and when, to help explain this section. For the month of April 2020, I spent a significantly higher than normal amount, £436 on groceries. This was weeks 2 to 5 of the Coronavirus Lockdown; the amount spent on treats and alcohol had increased significantly. A normal month for me is £250 to £300.

Back in the day, when I began my debt repayment, I made a big change to my grocery spending habits. I used to shop at Tesco. It was the closest supermarket to drive to and I used to work there, so had spent many years shopping there. Also Tesco was part of my life as since I was a child my mum shopped there. It was where I shopped when I took the housekeeping role on from her after she died. Shopping at Tesco was quite simply a habit and an expensive one at that. I was spending £120 per week on groceries.

I made the switch over to Aldi and immediately saved myself £40 a week. I know lots of people turn their nose up at Aldi, but I promise they are great, and are worth a try. The price difference is huge. Yes, there is less choice and the cashier whizzes your stuff through the check-out quicker than the speed of light, but it is worth it for a 30%+ weekly saving. Their fresh produce is great quality, often UK sourced (I know this as I work with them as one of my clients, their suppliers are farmers in Norfolk, chocolate makers in Cornwall, etc) and they do a simple 50% discount for soon-to-be out-of-date produce (that you can freeze for later - bonus).

Food money saving is a huge topic hence a whole chapter is dedicated to food in Chapter 8.

Eating Out and Takeaways

I love eating out. Not having to cook for myself is a huge treat, getting away from the routine of dinners (that are often not eaten) is brilliant. But they are a treat and expensive as cooking the same food at home will always cost you much less. There have been times in my life where I have ordered a takeaway twice a week, eight takeaways a month. At £30 a takeaway this is £240 per month. It can add up to a huge amount of money. I have mentioned emotional spending before, this is a clear example of emotional spending and eating wrapped up into the same thing. A significant spend on generally unhealthy food.

To save money I love to use voucher codes on meals out. I have a long list of recommended voucher codes apps to get some great deals and freebies on your takeaways and meals out.

Another idea that will save you on takeaways is to order a recipe box. I love Mindful Chef for its innovative healthy recipes. The recipe boxes cost around £25 to £30 for four meals a week. The food is amazing, restaurant quality and you get to make it yourself. Cooking is great for mental health and mind calming.

School Dinners

School dinners are free for all children up to end of year two currently. There are also free school dinners if you are on certain benefits. It is always worth checking with your school what costs you can get help with if income is low and you are struggling.

If you pay for school dinners it might be costing you around £13 a week per child, if you have three children year three or above this is £39 per week or £156 per month or two children is £26 per week or £104 per month. A huge cost on school dinners. And my boys often end up just choosing a baguette!

Sending the children in with a packed lunch is much better value. I wrote about making packed lunches for all three boys for five days for less than £10, using Aldi ingredients, £9.39 to be exact.

Car Costs

A car is an essential monthly cost to many of us. Do you own your car outright or have you bought on car finance with monthly payments? I have no objections to either of these options if you do it in the right way.
I have a Toyota Hybrid (a car that runs on self-charged electricity and unleaded fuel) CHR on car finance. I wanted a reliable and environmentally friendly car; I drive many miles around the country for my sons' football so cannot risk breaking down. In addition, I wanted lower fuel costs, so this was a good option (it costs around £40 to fill my tank for 400 miles, the old S Max equivalent was £70 for 500 miles). Plus, I did not have the £16k lying around to buy the car outright!

I chose to go for PCP finance. This is car finance scheme where I pay a monthly rental of the car for an agreed time period and interest rate. At the end of the payment period you either hand the car back to the car dealer or pay the balloon payment to own the car outright.

The car was priced at £24k. I paid an £8k deposit (via part-exchange) with £16k left on the PCP finance agreement. After paying £174 per month for 3 ½ years, will then be £9k left to pay. I can then choose between re-financing the remaining £9k, buying the car outright or handing it back to the Toyota dealer.

Just remember that everything is negotiable in a car purchase from the value of the trade-in car, to PCP interest rate, to cost of the car. I spent hours in that showroom negotiating every angle of the purchase. They got so annoyed with me, but I never gave up. I even walked out at one point and returned a few days later.

Of course, many people buy their car outright. More possible if you buy a second or third hand car. My dad always had the rule, buy at two years, sell at five years. I checked this rule recently with a mechanic friend, he suggested cars are much better built in modern times meaning you can go up to eight years with a car still being reliable provided you look after it.

When you buy a brand new car there is VAT to pay, a huge 20%. So that car I bought at £24k included nearly £5k of tax!! Often the best deals are with pre-registration cars or being the second owner. And then sell it before it starts costing you loads of money in repairs. I went to the launch party for heycar (where I met the very funny and tall men,

Vernon Kay and Harry Judd) and was really impressed with their concept of recommendations for used car sales. It takes away the embarrassing car salesmen in the showrooms. I will consider using them for my next car purchase to save lots of money compared to buying brand new.

Other Essential Costs- Money saving ideas

I've put a complete listing of all the recommendations I have for saving money in recommendations page on my website, just look for chapter 6, https://www.mrsmummypenny.co.uk/the-money-guide-to-transform-your-life-recommendations.

They are all products I use and love, and are sometimes affiliate links, where I receive a small fee if you become a customer. Fully disclosed if they are. But sometimes, they are just recommendations of companies I love.

A Page for Your Chapter 6 Notes

Chapter 7 - Family Life and Saving Money

There's no getting round it, if you have kids, it's expensive! Sometimes it can feel as though there's no end to a growing list of costs. In this chapter I offer some ideas as to how you can best save money. Getting a handle on these expenses and employing ideas to help you save money can eliminate stresses and help you to focus on what's really important, spending quality time with your family (and not sacrificing your own needs in order to make sure the children have everything they need).

My first son was born when I was 30. My pregnancy had been challenging, I had left my job at Tesco and was taking some time to regroup and recover after a tough five years of a relentless but extremely valuable career. My mental health was not in a great place. My maternity leave was spent planning a wedding. I had wanted to get married before our first baby arrived, a traditional view based on deep-seated beliefs from my mum who was also pregnant on her wedding day. We were married when I was 22 weeks pregnant. I have since explored this view and think: each to their own, you absolutely don't need to be married when you have children.

I had plenty of post wedding time to plan for the birth of my first baby. I felt like I knew nothing about being a first-time mum, except for the NCT classes that taught us what to expect from a C-section or natural childbirth and how to breastfeed. I knew nothing of the essential things you need for a baby. I went list crazy and bought everything, spending thousands on every single product that the John Lewis list told me to get. (I at least saved money by not getting it all from John Lewis, I shopped around!)

With hindsight and subsequent babies two and three I now realise that you do not need everything that John Lewis (or any other baby list retailer) tells you you need! In fact to help you out I have pulled together my own baby list, clearly listing the essentials and the nice to haves. Giving you ideas on how to save on everything. To download this document head to my book tools page on my website. https://www.mrsmummypenny.co.uk/the-money-guide-to-transform-your-life-tools

Having a family is expensive

There is no sugar coating this fact. Each stage of a child's life has its various expenses. The baby stage is ridiculously expensive with prams, nursery cost, endless nappies, baby wipes. Two washes a day of mum and baby clothes covered in puke.

Then maybe you go back to work, and you must pay for a full day of childcare costs. A full day costing anything from £50 to £100 depending on where you live in the UK. Then school comes along, school uniform, three, yes three pairs of school shoes per year. Activities start to kick in properly: football, dance, gymnastics, swimming, art classes, piano lessons.

Maybe you have a child who excels at a skill or sport, so you encourage them and spend way more on supporting their passion. They suddenly discover technology and want phones, games consoles, tablets, laptops. The teenage years hit, and clothes and branding become mega important.

Add in haircuts, opticians, medical costs, mental health support. The list goes on and on for the things that cost money for your beloved children.

My babies

I have three boys, I spent most of my 30s either being pregnant, on maternity leave or raising small children. What a decade!

Essential new baby list with costs

I wrote an essentials baby list based on my experience of having three babies and suggested some ways to save money on your essentials new baby list. My suggestions take the cost down from £1500 to less than £1000. You can find this list in my book tools page on my website. https://www.mrsmummypenny.co.uk/the-money-guide-to-transform-your-life-tools

Middle son Josh came along 23 months after Dylan. Having another boy was wonderful as I could reuse a lot of the stuff from Dylan. Bonus. Then little Jack arrived three years later. This is where things got expensive.

The family car was not big enough for a new baby, three-year-old, and five-year-old so I researched and bought a pre-registered S-Max. Just getting it as pre-reg, me being second owner, but with only 20 miles on the clock saved me £5k. Still, I spent £20k on a car. Having baby number three was my main motivation for our house extension, a project, as I explained in chapter 4 that we got completely carried away with.

I returned to work after Dylan & Josh baby when they were around nine months old. I had to go back to work, I was the breadwinner. My salary was crucial to pay the mortgage, the new bills and to pay off our debt. After Dylan was born I had to find a new job as I had taken redundancy whilst pregnant. Same with my middle child, my company went into administration whilst I was on maternity leave. Little Jack was born whilst I worked at EE so I had a well-paid maternity leave there, meaning I could take the full 12 months off (and give birth to Mrs MummyPenny at the same time!)

The boys grow so fast. I have loved spending quality time with them. Jack has had me around most of his life. A childminder looked after the older boys when they were little. I worked out that over the first seven years of being a mum I spend around £50k on childcare costs.

At the time of writing this book I have twelve, ten and seven-year-old boys. My eldest is a brilliant football player, he plays for Cambridge United football academy. This means training or games up to 5 days a week in Cambridge. We live in Hertfordshire, an hour's drive away. Josh is a mad scooter, BMX rider and loves to spend all weekend at scooter parks. Jack has not decided his passion yet, maybe football, maybe rugby, maybe cricket. I took him to a Cricket World cup event in London and the coaches all commented on his batting and bowling ability at age six.

Childcare costs

Childcare is a huge cost when the children are of pre-school age. Everybody has different ways of managing. I remember vetting seven nurseries whilst on maternity leave with my eldest. The one I chose (a huge chain nursery) 'felt' like the best (also £60 a day) but turned out not to be so great when DJ fell and smacked his nose on table edge, unsupervised. I wasn't informed until pick-up.

After that incident I quickly found a local childminder, via recommendation and an online search. We met, liked each other and DJ moved to his new childcare setting immediately. Everyone has a personal preference of nursery versus childminder versus nanny. I loved having a childminder for the personal home setting it gave all my boys. There were always lots of other children around and it was wonderful caring environment that gave me some flexibility. A childminder is also normally cheaper than a nursery.

I needed childcare for four to five days a week for the first eight years of parenthood (excluding maternity leaves). Once I found that childminder, I was sorted for childcare for all my boys until I no longer needed it. There were times when she had my one-year-old, four-year-old and six-year-old five days a week; those were expensive times, often costing more than £1000 a month. It felt like I was paying two mortgages for eight years.

I experimented dropping my hours to four days a week, or having the in-laws drive an hour to ours to look after the boys as ways of saving one day of childcare costs. But none of it really worked. Four days a week was the worst solution for a senior manager in a big company: I still did the five-day a week job but got paid 20% less (as many of you parents reading this will recognise). No thanks. The childminder was by the far the best solution for consistent childcare.

There is more help now to pay for childcare than there was when my boys were younger. At time of writing everyone gets 15 hours' free childcare and if you're working more than 16 hours a week you are eligible for 30 hours a week of childcare. There are also childcare voucher credits where you can get a tax refund to help pay for childcare, for more information head over to the government website for full details on help with childcare costs. Details in recommendations section on my website.

Life does get much easier once your children are at school, especially if you have a flexible employer who will let you work flexible hours around school drop-off or collection. My last employed job was with EE and I worked from home one/two days a week, this meant I could do the school run. If you don't have flexibility with your employer you will need wraparound care, a child minder that will do before and after childcare or there are breakfast clubs and after school clubs provided by your child's school.

Then there is the challenge of the 13 weeks of school holidays. Many parents must split their work holiday time separately to take turns looking after the children. Holiday clubs are a good value alternative to holiday childcare. I discovered the Sainsburys active kids club after many years of juggling the summer holidays or paying through the nose for expensive childcare. It worked out to be very good value. It was £15 a day per child for six hours of sporty care including food. You must get booked in early with these.

Just keep going until your child is around 12/13/14, whichever age you are comfortable with for them to be trusted and left at home by themselves. A 14-year-old teenager is legally allowed to babysit.

Then they go to school

Parents mostly do a little whoop when the children eventually start school the September of their fourth year. If you have a September to December baby it will cost you more in childcare as they will be nearly five by the time they start school. Speaking from personal experience here, with all three of my boys born in October and November. If you have a younger baby born in June, July, or August you will save money compared to the older children simply in lower childcare costs.

Off they toddle to school for six and a half hours a day and you could return to some sort of normality with your career if you choose to go back to work.

School Uniform

The initial cost of school is the school uniform. For primary school uniforms the supermarkets offer incredible value for money. And I have personally tried and tested them all. My favourite for value for money and great quality is Aldi. However, you must be super quick. The uniform arrives in store in July, and you need to be there early to grab the bits you want, when it's gone, it's gone. I love their polo tops (no, you really do not need an emblem polo top for primary school unless it's a posh school with uniform rules). In 2020 the polo tops are £1.50 for two tops, bargain. I grab five packets for each child, so I am not spending endless days washing clothes.

The jumpers are also great at Aldi, beware of the magic jumper disappearing trick, my boys lose at least four jumpers per year at primary school, despite them being named. Hey Ho. I also get the plain black or grey socks. Always buy the same colour so they are easier to match up after washing.

I head to Asda for shorts and trousers. They are made from sturdy material, especially on the knees. Asda is where I go if I need top-ups (jumpers normally) during the school year.

School shoes, what a minefield and believe me I have tried everywhere. I spent a few years only buying from Clarks at a huge cost, £30-40 per pair. My shoes often cost less than this!! I have shopped at Sports Direct for trainer style black shoes and we have tried supermarket shoes. To be honest, all the shoes just get worn out and ripped and torn quickly. Children just burn through shoes with their playground football, running races, picking at shoes at school when bored. I suggest if you are going to replace every term, yes you heard that right, replace every term, go for cheaper. My preferred shop is always Sports Direct where I know I can get a half decent pair of shoes for around £20. So that was £60 a term for my boys when they were at primary school, £180 a year JUST ON SCHOOL SHOES.

PE kits often must have the school emblem on them, shorts, T-shirt. You can get these from the second-hand shop at your school, every school has them.

Secondary School Uniforms

Secondary school is a whole new world for the cost of uniform. My eldest needed a huge list of stuff and it all came from one shop with a total monopoly on prices meaning it was expensive. How I cursed and moaned about the unfairness. DJ goes to a boys' school (non-paid for), but this is normal practice for secondary schools after checking with friends in other schools and all over the country.

We needed a blazer, tie, hoody, rugby shirt, PE T-shirt, PE shorts, joggers, basketball kit, high-performance sport T-shirt, hockey stick, rugby boots, indoor trainers, running trainers. This is extensive as Dylan plays in the basketball team and high-performance sports team, but I have easily spent £400 on school uniform bits. My only savings was to get white shirts and black trousers from Asda.

We also needed a scientific calculator, geometry set, clear pencil case, highlighters, glue, black non obviously branded coat. We found proper bargains in WH Smith of all places, a shop I rarely go to, but they had everything we needed with such savings in August when we did the shopping.

School Trips and After school activities

I do not spend too much on school trips, the schools are generally great at keeping the costs down and supporting costs with internal funding. Always inform the school if you are in financial hardship. The school may offer a payment scheme or help towards payment. If the trip is supporting the curriculum (most should be) parents should not have to pay – although the reality is if enough parents don't pay the trip may not go ahead.

There are school trips for my boys once a year. Swimming is often something that you need to pay for as well as any after school clubs. But many are free of charge. We have sports options at my school that are around £5 per session for two hours after school. There is art, drama, music lessons (you pay for these normally). If your child is chosen for a school team there will be games that you might have to transport them too. Every school has a different policy.

Secondary schools often have a minibus to take teams to after-school games. Year six and secondary schools are when school trips can get expensive. Everything is of course voluntary, but I would feel awful guilt if my child could not go on a trip when all his friends were.

PGL trips happen in year six and year seven and can cost anything from £100 to £300. We have had letters from school for Year eight trips to Los Angeles and Costa Rica for PE and Geography respectively, but at £2,000 each I have said to Dylan "No Way!" I would rather put that money towards a family holiday.

Travelling to School

Hopefully, you live within walking or cycling distance of your children's school. We do for primary but not for secondary. My eldest gets the train to school, two stops away, this costs £70 every half term. £400ish a year to get to school. Ouch. This is the cheapest I can get it with a young person's railcard.

The school bus is another option but again it can be expensive, sometimes more expensive than the train. Or maybe you could drive them to school.

Sporting Activities and Clubs

There is a huge array of privately run activities for children. Especially those who display a talent in something. I will always encourage this for each of my children and in no way resent the amount of money it might cost for them to follow their dream.

Football

I know a lot about football, having three boys. My eldest has played since he was three years old and is now an U13 Cambridge United Academy Football player with an exciting future ahead. So much has been spent on football over the years, endless pairs of football boots (Adidas please offer us a sponsorship deal!!), football kits, goalie gloves (he's not even a goalie), shin pads, warm coats, kit bags.

Then there is petrol money I spend on getting him to training three to four times a week and a game anywhere in the country at the weekend, anywhere from Liverpool to Bournemouth. He also goes on two tours a year to Germany at £250ish for each trip. It is a cost of around £2000 per year. But if he makes it, he has promised to buy me a house!

Grass Roots Football

Most football for children is at grass roots level, the games at your local park. Again, there is still the cost of kits, boots, and annual subscriptions (at least I do not have to pay for coaching in the football academy system).

Swimming

Confession time. I have never paid for a swimming lesson for any of my boys. We regularly go to the swimming pool and have a holiday every year with a swimming pool, so I have taught the boys how to swim myself. They are all strong swimmers, totally self-taught and taught by mum. Huge amount of money saved there. Like the football, if you child excels at swimming then there are huge travel costs getting your children to and from swimming galas.

Dancing

My boys do not do dance, but I have so many friends with children who do. And this is a hugely expensive activity for children. Weekly lessons, dance outfits, ballet, tap, modern dance shoes. It is as expensive, if not more so than football! I have a few friends whose children have appeared in the local pantomime. The children get paid a tiny amount and the parents spend a fortune on transport and pocket money for snacks.

Beavers, Scouts, Brownies & Guides

My boys haven't taken part in these clubs, not through want of trying, the waiting lists were so long to get them in. These clubs provide incredible opportunities to learn new skills, sports and giving back to the local community. An added bonus being many days out and camping trips. The membership fees are good value too.

There are many others to mention, but that's a whole book' worth!

Family Holidays

I love a holiday and prioritise saving for holidays above many other things. I love creating the memories and for the boys to experience different cultures and countries. So far, we have been to Spain, France, Corsica (French island but closer to Italy), Portugal, plus many visits to Cornwall and Norfolk. We have had holidays every year even when in debt. I got the mum guilt and we ended up further in debt to pay for the holidays.

But I do have some holiday recommendations that will save you money.

Book a France Gîte

This was a wonderful holiday when Jack was just six months old. Dylan and Josh were five and three . We drove to the Eurotunnel and then drove to Brittany in France. It was a nine-hour journey in total. But we had everything we needed packed into the car that you need for small people and a baby.

My friend Carolyn Haycox runs the most beautiful holiday location with Gîtes named after fruits. The grounds are huge with all sort of games and sports for the children, plus a swimming pool. She also has chickens, ducks, cats and cows in the field next door. It is idyllic.

A Gîte for four people is around 1200 Euros for a week in the summer holidays, as of 2020. This is a self-catering price, so you need to allow for food on top. Add the cost of fuel and Euro-tunnel tickets. Maybe another £200.

You could totally do this holiday for less than £2000.

Go to Centerparcs in France or Holland

I did a slightly crazy thing and agreed to go on Good Morning Britain for a feature where they would find a last-minute holiday for the first week of the summer holiday in 2018. Off we went at 5am to the ITV studio in White City to spend the morning. Simon Calder, the very lovely travel expert was there to find us a deal. I asked for a week somewhere hot for two adults and three children including food for less than £2000. Haha. He shook his head at me, I am not sure this is possible Lynn, on air, with Ben Shepherd chuckling away.

He tried to find us a deal, Spanish hotels that he had been to, including flights were coming out at more like £4000! He found us a week but flying from Manchester, leaving that day for £3000. Then we had a brainwave before the show was over.

Simon loves a Centerparcs holiday and recommended the Les Bois-Franc location, not far from Paris, a simple drive from Calais via the ferry. He recommended to avoid the Eurotunnel that year as the air conditioning kept breaking! He found us a lovely centre parks cottage that slept 6 for 1400 Euros for one week. There was a bit of mess-up in the booking and he managed to get us a bonus apology 200 Euro voucher to spend when we were there! The ferry ticket was free as I exchanged some Tesco Clubcard vouchers.

The boys loved it at Centerparcs. Me not so much. It was self-catering, so I had to cook all the breakfasts, lunches and dinner, unless we went to onsite restaurants, which were so expensive. Plus, they wanted to do lots of activities that cost a lot of money. Badminton 16 Euro a pop, that kind of thing. Plus, the bikes, we all hired bikes, another 200 Euro.

We ended up spending around 1000 Euro for the week including food and activities (after our 200 Euro voucher was redeemed). And this was even with me doing a big Aldi shop and taking that with us.

So yes, this holiday cost around 2500 Euros, plus fuel to get there of around £100. The boys loved it and would go back. I wouldn't as I didn't get any rest. They loved the water park, and it was amazing for the first three days, but I was over it by days four to seven, please no more water parks.

Mark Warner Holidays

Hear me out on this one! Mark Warner are well known for being on the expensive side for holidays. But not so much if you can wangle a term time holiday. Or maybe a week with a couple of inset days meaning you are missing just three days of school. I have done this twice! P.S. I am not promoting taking time off school for a holiday and you may well get a fine from your local education authority.

I took the boys to Corsica (resort now sadly closed) as a single mum. It cost around £500 each for a week and this included everything, hotel, flights, transfers. food, wine, all sports were included (and the range is incredible, tennis, wind surfing, paddle boarding, table tennis, volleyball, mountain biking and more). The price also included childcare and exercise classes. The only extras were two evening meals during the week, the spa and beach bar drinks. Other spending money was minimal.

It was the most amazing holiday that we will go back to again and again, albeit to a different location (Sardinia or Greece). It was a super relaxed holiday, the boys made so many friends and I could read my books, sunbathe and do all the sports. It is the best holiday as a single parent, you make friends with the other parents drinking the included wine.

The Most Expensive Holiday Ever - 2 weeks self-catering in Spain

This may surprise you as I thought it would be cheaper. We did two weeks in Southern Spain with friends. It was August so flights and accommodation were at their peak costing around £2k for five people.

We spent so much money on eating out, food at the apartment, drinks from the bar during the daytime, two visits to water park. Plus, car hire. In total we spent nearly

£5k in two weeks! And I had to do a lot of the cooking. For a relaxing holiday I need a break from cooking!

UK Holidays

We have had many UK holidays. I am lucky to be from Penzance, Cornwall, where my sister still lives. Meaning we always have a place to stay in Cornwall. Daily trips to the beach are the cost of a picnic lunch and parking for the day, with the obligatory ice-cream (Jelberts in Newlyn is the best).

I adore the sea and the beach and must return to living near the sea one day. The sea makes me happy, encourages creativity and relaxation. I spent my first 18 years by the sea, I adore it.

We have tried out caravan holidays, at Haven-type resorts. Always good fun for the kids, especially when you go with a group of friends. Watch them spend a small fortune in the arcade, where, according to a friend who worked there, Haven make a huge chunk of their profits.

I have booked Airbnb accommodation in Norfolk for long days on the golden sands, spotting seals. We have stayed in Wells-next-the-sea, which is the most beautiful place, on a par with Cornwall and easier to reach from London. It could be where I end up living, once the boys have flown the nest.

Airbnb is a fab option to save money on a holiday. We booked a beautiful cottage in Norfolk that slept four people and it was £600 for a week, in the summer holidays, the hottest week of 2019. In October half term we booked a chalet to sleep four of us and it was £50 a night!

Days Out with the Children

We love a day out exploring places of interest. As the boys get older tastes change and they become less likely to want to go to places that I do. Although I have gotten good at finding places where there is one thing they like, and one thing I like. Cambridge for example. We can take the train there with my network railcard; it costs around £10 to get all four of us there. We go to the swimming pool with water slides in the morning and then go to botanical gardens in the afternoon with a picnic bought from the Sainsburys local near the swimming pool!

Here is a selection of my favourite days out with money saving ideas

The Zoo

I have lots close by in Hertfordshire, but my favourites are London Zoo, Shepreth Zoo and Paradise Park. London Zoo is expensive if you just rock up and buy a ticket. But be clever and use your train tickets to get buy one get one free tickets. You need to print off a voucher before you leave home from the website -Days Out Guide, London Zoo is just one of many 2 for 1 offers, look at what else you can do. London Aquarium, London Eye or the London Dungeons are a few ideas. So much more to choose from too.

Shepreth is a local zoo in Cambridgeshire. So much cheaper than London Zoo and they do a lot for animal conservation. They are located next to the train station and if you get the train there, direct from London on the Cambridge route, or just 40 minutes for us, there is a discount off your entry tickets.

Paradise Park is a Hertfordshire Zoo in Broxbourne. And there are often voucher codes available to get half price entry. Keep an eye on sites like Vouchercodes, Groupon and Buy A Gift.

Take a picnic with you to cut back on the food costs and try to avoid the shop at the end. A tricky one is that! I tend to say to them that they have a £5 limit to what they can buy from the shops of tat. Helps them with maths skills too and understanding the value of things. No Jack, I am not paying £35 for a cuddly gorilla!

Cinema

We all adore going to the cinema, a fun afternoon for all three boys. The boys love a wide range of films that I also like, Avengers, The Greatest Showman, Sonic (okay I hated that one), James Bond.

We either have the local council run cinema that is much cheaper to go to, around £25 for 4 of us. Or we go to Cineworld, with more comfy seats and bigger screens, better audio etc. I get 40% off our Cineworld tickets by having a Kids Pass subscription, link in recommendations page on website.

This is a discount club that gives money off all cinema chains, family food and family days out. It costs £2.99 a month. Well worth it as we go the cinema at least once a month.

Using the Kids Pass means that tickets for the four of us cost around £24. And we take in popcorn, drinks and a tub of ice-cream that we buy en route from Tesco! Sneaky.

Trampoline Park

Another favourite for the boys, or any child, is the trampoline park. But they do range in price. We have found a local authority not for profit park in Welwyn Garden City, where is it £8 per child when you go at off peak times. Better Extreme is the name, there are a few of them around the country.

Free days out and about

You need to have a big list of ideas for free days out to save cash at the weekends and during the holidays. Here are some of the things that we do regularly.

Nature Trail

You can find nature wherever you live, even in inner-city built-up areas. Create a list of animals, birds, insects, flowers and trees for your child to spot when out for your walk. Make a list of 20 to spot. It can be a fun competition between children, and a learning activity as well. Even when I go out for a walk by myself, I do this. I have a four-mile walk from Knebworth to Old Knebworth to Rabley Heath back to Knebworth and on that route are horses, pigs, sheep, cows, cats, dogs, chickens, so many birds, butterflies, rabbits, even an occasional rat!

Geocaching

Geocaching is a virtual treasure hunt. Have a look at the website, as listed in my recommendations page to find trails near you. You attempt to find the treasure chest and can take one item of treasure. Just be sure to take an item with you to pop in the chest to keep it full of bits for other children to take. This reminds me of the Duke of Edinburgh award walks I used to do aged 14 with a map and compass, where we always got lost or ended up walking through bogs and marshes of West Cornwall.

Spend time near water

I love to spend time near water and have found so many places in Hertfordshire to do this. There are many splash parks which the younger children love. You can find these all over the country and are free. But even better is finding a glorious and clean and safe river to dip your toes into. But the ultimate is a day at the beach and seaside. Totally free if you take a picnic lunch and you have somewhere with free parking.

Ideas at home

When the weather is cold and raining it is more of a challenge to keep the children amused. What about these ideas...

Recycling challenge

Collect up your clean recycling for a few days. Give the children some Sellotape, scissors, duct tape and felt tips pens and let them loose with their creativity. Make a castle, or a robot or a dolls house, wherever the imagination takes you or them.

Treasure Hunt

We love a treasure hunt on a rainy day. Each child has a list of ten things that they need to find in the house, a red crayon, a birthday card, a fork, a book, a DVD, one black sock, nail varnish, 2p coin etc. Amend for each child an see who can collect the items the quickest.

Cleaning and De-cluttering

Is this woman mad, I hear you say! No, we have cleaning challenges in our house. We have recently tackled the entire house and decluttered, cleaned out every single room and cupboard. The garage was super fun for the boys. I hired a skip and they had a wonderful time chucking everything into the skip. Yes, the entire contents of the garage that we have not used for more than a year!

My eldest son enjoys cleaning, so I set him little challenges of hoovering the artificial grass or mopping the floor. We all take turns, I do most of it to be honest. But it's good. It teaches them valuable life lessons and especially for boys that mum is not there to be a slave doing everything.

Lego blanket

If your house is anything like ours, you will have boxes of Lego. We occasionally spread out a blanket and tip out the Lego and create whatever comes to mind. We lost the instructions and boxes for the Lego kits long ago but like to make new things. A prison, or a zoo, or a house with multiple rooms or a car. Lego is totally my favourite children's toy. Likewise, for my boys and it lasts for years and years.

Crafty box

I have a box in which I collect crafty bits, coloured card, sharpies, stickers, pompoms, glue, paint, glitter. We will have a crafting time and create birthday cards, posters, whatever comes to mind. But beware of the glitter. It gets everywhere!

A Page for Your Chapter 7 Notes

Chapter 8 – Food Money Saving

After mortgage or rent, food spend is normally the biggest household expense. In the days when I paid little attention to spending, I could easily spend £600 a month on groceries and takeaways combined in those days of emotional spending mixed in with depression.

I remember working full time at EE, working four days a week in London, rarely seeing my children. I was stressed out at work and stressed out at home. The boys had been fed dinner at the childminders and the easiest solution for me was a takeaway for dinner. I was too tired to do anything else.

The consequence was physical and mental issues. The unhealthy food caused my body and mind way more stress with the levels of sugar and fat and I gained a lot of weight. And the cost was wholly unacceptable.

Food is a trigger issue for most of us. We believe we're making rational decisions about our spending, but often we're not. Understanding your food shopping habits more and making a few simple changes can save you an enormous amount of money. In this chapter I'll share with you some of the best and easiest recipes that can save you money, help you and your family to eat healthier for less and transform eating back into the pleasurable shared experience we'd all like it to be.

My relationship with food

I love food, at some points in my life too much. I have always associated food with emotion. Celebrations, happiness, anger, sadness. I have always turned to food in times of high emotion. I am an emotional eater and spender.

The two are closely linked and the triggers are the same, sometimes the emotional reactions mean a £20 spend on treat food, which I might then binge on. I am then wracked with guilt, and pledge to be better the next day, except I am not, or the next day. I get caught up in a cycle of months of binge eating and spending. I put on weight and my bank account dwindles.

But the great thing is, as I get older and with plenty more life experience and therapy in my toolbox, I recognise that I lean towards emotional eating and spending. And I feel more able to keep it in check. Of course, it rears its head in difficult times. I binge ate my way through the Autumn/Winter of 2019/2020 and put on 2 stone in weight. The lockdown of 2020 and the separation from my ex was the trigger I need to stop the behaviour and to look after my body with the fuel I was putting into it.

Saving money on your food bill

I think the key to saving money on food is meal planning. This will be your friend and your key to saving money. Before you hit the shop plan your meals for the week: breakfast, lunch, dinner and snacks. Think about your diary too, are there any nights where you are out, or have people over for food?

Use a meal planner to work out your meals for the week. I have created this template for you, to download this document head to my book tools page on my website. https://www.mrsmummypenny.co.uk/the-money-guide-to-transform-your-life-tools and have included a weeks' worth of ideas to feed healthy food to a family of four, costing less than £40. Including Taco Tuesday, home-made pizza and cottage pie. It is based on an article I wrote for The Sun in July 2020.

I have a stock of classic meals for the boys that I rotate. It is not a huge variety of meals, but I know that they all like the food and will eat it.

My Standard list consists of:

- Chicken, Pepper and Onion Fajitas (I buy the Fajita pack from Aldi with tortillas, spice and salsa)
- Beef Tacos with salad, cheese, and salsa (I buy the Taco pack from Aldi with taco shells, spices and salsa)
- Roast Chicken – I love the roast in a bag chickens from Aldi, £4ish and the chicken cooks moistly or push the boat out and get a free-range organic chicken as per my meal planner in my book tools on my website. With roast potatoes and vegetables, fresh or frozen.
- Chicken Nuggets, Chips and Veg – I always have a stock of chicken nuggets, dippers, or popcorn chicken in the freezer. Perfect served with frozen chips and frozen veg or baked beans.

- Sausages and mash – The best sausages are from my village butchers Trussells The Knebworth sausage is literally a banger. I either make mash or if I cannot be bothered, I use frozen mash from Aldi (which to be honest the boys prefer!).
- All-day breakfast – A classic that the boys love. A plate of sausage, bacon, eggs, mushrooms, beans, toast.
- Homemade pizza or frozen pizza – we have made homemade pizza a few times. Not going to lie it's time consuming, but it is lots of fun, and quite enjoyable to take out any anger feelings on a piece of dough. We top the pizza with anything from the fridge we can lay hands on: cheese, bits of ham, tomatoes, peppers, onions, meatballs, bacon. I also ensure there is always a frozen pizza in the freezer for 'cannot be bothered to cook' emergencies.
- Spaghetti Bolognese – I make a beautiful spaghetti Bolognese, I have also included the link to the recipe from my website. The recipe says it is for the pressure cooker, but the same recipe works on the hob, just cook it for a bit longer.
- Hot dogs – I know, they are cheap and nasty, but the boys love them! Cheapo (cows genitals) sausages in hot dog rolls with mustard and ketchup. Dinner done in less than five minutes!
- Snacky buffet selection – This is a rustle up of anything we might have in the fridge. I might make some potato salad, boiled potatoes with mayo and a few spring onions. I will do bowls of green salads. Some chicken on a plate, some grated cheese, crisps

in a bowl. The boys love to pick and have whatever they want.

- Pancakes – The ultimate breakfast. We adore pancakes and make them at least once a week. I use the Nigella crepe method. 150g of plain flour, 350 ml of milk, one egg, butter to cook. So good. We fill them with chocolate spread and mini "smarshmellows" (as Jack calls them still) if I have them.

The big weekly shop

Now that you know what you are going to be cooking for the week from your meal planner you can write a shopping list. And it is essential to go shopping with a list to save money and stick to that list. Another little tip I have picked up: use one of those half-sized trolleys. Less room to fit everything in! And check your freezer before you leave as there might be some things in there written on your list!

I like shopping at Aldi. The stores are smaller and there is less choice, another way to save money. Most of their products are own brand, hence the cheaper prices. The meat and fresh produce are great quality and mostly UK produced (I have met all of the Aldi buyers at their Christmas events and love to talk about where their produce comes from and the relationships they have with their producers).

I have done lots of work with Aldi over the years with Mrs MummyPenny. They were the first big brand that I landed work with back in 2016. I have worked on so many campaigns with Aldi, bank holiday cocktails, summer camping trips, mother's day, back to university, packed lunched for under £10, festival jewellery, budget make-up, £90 serum vs. £6 serum, plus much more. This work has been in every newspaper in the land, the packed lunchbox post was seen by millions of people, my second viral piece of work (after the £16k debt story in The FT and The Sun).

Yes, they do pay me or gift me products to produce content for them, but I also love the brand and would only rave about a brand that I genuinely love and use. And I spend £100 there every two weeks with my bi-weekly big shops!

The special buys aisle is always a treasure trove, although one to avoid when you are looking to save money. On a recent shop I picked up reusable make-up pads (£3.99), beautiful red lipstick (£2.99), a candle (£3.99 but a dupe of Yankee candles) and a fluffy blanket for £1.50.

I also love the booze aisle. Aldi gin is award winning and amazingly cheap. The Gordon's copy is £9.99 a bottle. I also love the pink gin and many of the flavoured gins, Seville orange is a good one. And their wines are fabulous. I have a favourite sweet wine called Moscato, from California, it is less than £5and it is the best.

Aldi and Lidl shopping will save you money compared to the likes of Tesco, Sainsburys and Asda. But this only works if you have one near to you. Their network is ever expanding so hopefully you will have one soon if not now.

Baking with Mummy

We love to bake. It is a fun activity to do at home to spend time together and we get yummy sweet treats at the end of it. I have so many tried and tested recipes to share with you so you can get baking with your children.

Make sure that you have a baking stash in the store cupboard, with plain flour, self-raising flour, baking powder, bicarb of soda, stork/butter, and eggs. Also, good to have in are vanilla, chocolate chips, raisons, oats, syrup, cocoa powder and brown sugar.

All these recipes mentioned can be found in my chapter 8 recommendations on my website. https://www.mrsmummypenny.co.uk/the-money-guide-to-transform-your-life-recommendations.

Flapjacks

I found an amazing recipe for Flapjacks with a touch of lemon rind and ginger powder. There are oats, syrup, soft brown sugar, butter, raisins. Totally unhealthy but so yummy. One to make.

Marble Cake

We make this one all the time, using the BBC Good Food recipe. It's so easy that the boys can now make it by themselves. Although I tend to not let them swirl it at the prebaking stage, as we end up with a brown mess rather than a marble effect.

Victoria Sponge

Many a recipe tried here but the best has to be from Faith Archer, and it is an award-winning recipe (village country show!). Tried and tested for my 43rd birthday, a total winner.

Scones

Another thing I have tried to make in the past and have failed. Again, Faith comes to the rescue with a wonderful recipe for scones. I baked these for VE day with lashings of clotted cream and strawberry jam. They were amazing and so reminded me of home, Cornwall, and a cream tea.

Chocolate Chip cookies

Whenever I say, 'Boys shall we bake?', the boys ask to bake these. The best chocolate chip cookies in the world, courtesy of my amazing baker friend Emma Wright (you'll always be Chizlett to me!).

This recipe makes loads, maybe 30 cookies, so you pop the ones you do not bake into the freezer for the next day. But I can guarantee that once baked they will be scoffed within five minutes. They are amazing. I can easily put away four in one sitting. I like to make them with a mixture of white and milk chocolate chips.

Packed Lunches or School Dinners

School dinners are free for every child until they reach year 3, so you may as well do this. But then they cost from Year 3 onwards, unless you are eligible for free school meals (normally if you are on universal credit you can claim free school dinners). The school dinners are £2.60 per day at our Primary school - pricey. I would rather the boys had packed lunches. At least I know what is going into the packed lunch box and that they will eat it (hopefully).

I have got the cost of packed lunch right down to less than £10 per week for three boys for five days. 15 packed lunches for less than £10. Here is how I did it, an excerpt from the article read by millions of people across the world when the story went viral in Sept 2019.

Lynn's lunch meal plan

Day 1: Wrap with chicken & mayo, apple, home-made egg muffin with feta and kale, carrot sticks, crackers – 61p per child

Day 2: Sandwich with egg mayo, satsuma, yoghurt, kale crisps, cucumber – 61p per child

Day 3: Sandwich with jam, banana, carrot sticks, home-made flap jack, yogurt –47p per child

Day 4: Sandwich with chicken and cucumber, apple, pepper strips, home made egg muffin with feta and kale, crackers –72p per child

Day 5: Wrap with chicken & mayo, satsuma, cucumber slices, home made flap jack and home made kale crisps – 72p per child

Total: £3.13 per child and £9.39 for all three children

Egg muffins recipe

These are so lovely, and super healthy and easy to make. This recipe makes six, so covers two days of lunches.
- 3 eggs
- 50g feta cheese
- 25g chopped up kale

Break the eggs into a bowl and mix in the chopped kale and feta. Add the mixture to six muffin cases. Bake at 180 degrees in fan over/190 regular over for 25 minutes. They are very nice warm, but keep for a few days in the fridge.

Takeaways and Eating Out

I love to eat out and to get a takeaway, but I do try to limit this. Particularly when financial times are tough, and I am needing to save money. There have been times when we have ordered two takeaways a week as a family. Costing a huge £200 a month, just on takeaways! This was during sad emotional times when I could not be bothered to shop or cook so the only way to eat was to order takeaways.

A nice way to live and still treat yourself is to still have the takeaway but less often, maybe once a week on Friday night or you could make your own fakeaway.

Here are a few ideas that I do that go down well with the children.

Chinese Chicken and rice

I buy a pack of this from Aldi, chicken strips with peppers, spring onions, pre-cut. Along with a sauce. I serve with the brown rice from a packet, that takes 2 mins in the microwave. This food tastes just like the Chinese takeaway version and cost so much less. And the children all love it! (Maybe not the peppers!)

Mexican quesadillas, tortillas, Fajitas, tacos, nachos.

The boys all adore Mexican food, every type I make and give them to try they love it. I think it is the act of building your own food from the selection of meat, salad, cheese, sour cream, salsa and avocado that they love. The ability to create your own food tastes is a big deal to child craving some control.

DJ will try a bit of everything, whilst the other boys will just add the meat and veg mix plus salsa, maybe a few salad leaves.

Pad Thai

I adore Pad Thai and Wagamama is totally my favourite chain restaurant for a treat, alas it's very expensive. Our last trip cost around £60 for four of us eating, ouch!

I have found a great pad Thai kit from the Co-op. It costs £2ish and comes with the spices and noodles. All you then need to add is choice of meat, vegetables and beansprouts.

Fish n Chips

This is a tricky one to replicate and personally I cannot find a chippy better than Rowes in Stevenage. It is the best! If pushed I would say that the Youngs Fish from the freezer section is very good, the jumbo fish fingers are great for a fish finger sandwich. And for chips, just cut up small potatoes into quarters, coat them in a bit of oil (I like rapeseed oil), salt and pepper and roast for 25 mins on 200 (fan oven).

Healthy Eating

Making nutritious and healthy food is important to me and to my family. DJ is an academy football player and needs a huge number of good calories for the training or games five days a week. And I am super keen to get fruit and veg into them via any means possible.

Healthy eating does not have to be expensive, in fact if you choose a vegetarian diet then your shopping will come down in price! Meat and fish are expensive, even from Aldi.

There are certain vegetables that are more filling and meatier in texture. Jackfruit is lovely and tastes like pulled pork. I love aubergines cut in half and roasted in the over with a bit of oil. Cauliflower is wonderful roasted with a few random spices from the stock cupboard (I would mix up cumin, paprika, chilli powder and some oil and plaster the thickly sliced cauliflower).

Eggs are an incredibly versatile and healthy ingredient and are much cheaper than meat. Although try to buy free range. I like to buy from local friends with chickens, these are the best eggs by far! A poached egg with salmon and avocado is the best. A fried egg and bacon sandwich is a winner for the boys. A boiled egg with soldiers is a perfect breakfast, as is scrambled eggs.

I have discovered a new love for Tofu, covered in cornflour and then fried in Rapeseed oil, it's lovely with vegetables and rice, maybe a bit of Teriyaki sauce.

I must add that we are not healthy all of time, there is normally a treat food for dinner once or twice a week. I have been known to get Rustlers burgers for the boys for an easy treat dinner, they love them so much!!

A Page for Your Chapter 8 Notes

Chapter 9 - Healthy Body & Mind

I truly believe that we should not just work on a healthy attitude and behaviours with money, we should also focus on healthy body and mind. If we have all three working in partnership then life should be good, balanced, and you will feel more in control.

In this section I'll share with you what has worked for me over the years to achieve a good balance of a healthy body and mind, which in turn has led to a better and healthier approach towards money. Different things work for different people and my main advice is to encourage you to try different things and go with your instinct on what works for you.

Healthy Mind

I will start with the healthy mind and will share some of things I have been through and great coping mechanisms I've learned through them. Having a healthy mind is probably the most important aspect of you as a person. Things are thrown at us, life really is a rollercoaster, with the ups and downs sent to test us. How we deal with those ups and downs forms our outlook on life our personality, beliefs and emotions.

Did you know that you money beliefs start to form at the age of seven. Those experiences as a child not only form your adult personality, but also the way you behave with money.

Events effect how the brain motor neurons are connected and formed as children. I learnt as a child that I had to work for my money, and I then had the freedom to do what I wanted with that money. I always worked from the age of 14 and did as many hours as I could.

At 16 when my mum died, I was floored, emotionally and personality wise. I spent the subsequent years abusing my body, mind, and money. I was on self-destruct mode for many years, despite just getting the A-levels I needed to get into a decent university. I ran away from my home, Cornwall, two years after my mum died, to London for university.

I remember clearly the day my grant cheque money came through (I studied in the 90s, in the days when you could get a grant for university to cover some living expenses and the degree course itself was free of charge). I headed straight into Uxbridge town centre, rubbing my hands with glee and £700 in the bank account (it was paid at the start of each of the three terms). I went straight to Top Shop and bought £100 of clothes and then went to Dixons (remember them!) and spent £200 on a new stereo. Never mind that my £700 grant was meant to feed me and pay for nights out for the next three months.

I then proceeded to drink and party my way through my first year of university. I had a great time, and a sad time. I did not study, I was not focused on lectures, and with a maths degree with 16 hours of lectures a week this was wasteful. Drinks were £1 each in the student union where we lived every Wednesday and Friday night, dancing to Pulp, Take That and Baby D.

And then, eight months after university had begun, I got a phone call early on 27th May 1996 that my dad had died. My security was completely ripped away, and my mental health was destroyed. Soon after this event was when a university friend told me I had to get counselling which my personal tutor quickly sorted out for me and my life in therapy began.

Over my 20s and 30s I dipped in and out of therapy of different kinds. Counselling, self-discovery courses (that felt like a cult), psychotherapy, life coaching. I have tried everything, each helped in its own unique way. Well sort of.

With counselling or therapy, you do need to find the right person, and you need to be in the right mindset to accept the guidance and help. But the fact that you addressed you needing counselling is the best start.

My most recent exploration into understanding my behaviours has been from taking a course called Emotionally Wealthy People. A ten-day online course using Zoom classes and course notes.

This was a life-changing course where I felt like I had all my childhood, previous life beliefs and needs thrown up into the air. During the course I began the process to rebuild it all back up again in a balanced and caring way.

The course is focused on money beliefs and learnings, but the strategy learned can be applied to family life, relationships, work life, everything. We learnt the theory and then spent the following few days journaling our thoughts on the life needs and how they impact us. Along with journaling the coping strategies that we were taught,

I love to learn new and revolutionary strategies to help my mind to process the daily things sent to test us. I hugely recommend counselling and internally focused courses. They really are a life saver.

Healthy Body

A healthy body is incredibly important. The basics of survival is to have a healthy mind and body, without these you will not survive. And looking after your physical being is important.

I spent much of my adult life destroying my body. Early trauma in my life caused an eating disorder, and weight issues from age of 16 to 38. My poison was binge eating and I could very easily consume 5000 calories of food in one sitting. I would eat a whole tub of Haagen Dazs, a big bar of chocolate and crisps. And then again, the next day and the next. It's clear how I ended up at 16 stones at my heaviest.

I am 5ft 6in and my weight should be somewhere between 9 and 11 stones. 16 stone was clinically obese.

I spent much of my life yoyo dieting, going to Slimming World for a few months, losing a few stone, then putting it back on again when the bingeing would start again. My emotional eating was harming my body in a huge way. The constant yo-yo-ing likely did me more harm than anything.

My 40th birthday was the event that prompted me to sort out my weight issues and I booked myself in for hypnotherapy with Heather Hall in Hemel Hempstead. After a few sessions, my subconscious had been re-programmed and I stopped with the binge eating. A nutrition expert friend helped me to devise a super clean eating detox, and I shed 3 stones in about 6 months.

I make it sound simple, and it was. I dealt with the emotional side of my eating and the practical side of eating, relearning the right foods to eat and I was fixed.

Of course, I slip back into old habits occasionally, where there is big emotion, but I can normally get it under control. The only time I did not was the winter of 2019 when I was going through a complicated and emotionally destructive divorce. I turned to my vices of binge eating sugary and fatty food. And I did it every day for three months, the result was a two stone weight gain.

Once I shed the ex, I also very quickly shed the excess weight and within two months it was gone. My big life lesson is that recognising when I am unhappy helps me to keep my weight under control.

Healthy eating

I love to experiment with healthy eating. And am very much enjoying the vegan dishes I get from Mindful chef. Mindful Chef is a weekly subscription box with healthy food. All the ingredients and recipes are provided. Every meal, and I mean every single meal has been amazing, from teriyaki tofu, to cottage pie (with leeks, celeriac rather than mash), to stir fries. Every meal has at least four of your five a day veg as well. To save money I order two lots of meals for two. This gives me four sometimes six meals per week as often the portions are huge so I might split a meal for two into three portions and keep them for the next two days. This costs around £25 per week, if you order fish and meat it is more like £30 a week.

I also practise daily fasting. I do not eat in the morning despite getting up at 5 to 6am! My first meal is normally a small lunch at 1pmish. I will then have something bigger rich in vegetables for dinner at least five times a week. This often means I am cooking different things for the boys than me, but honestly, they are not keen on my vegan creations!! I recently bought some vegan grated cheese for cheesy chips for the boys, Jack said "Mummy this cheese tastes funny, get the normal cheese next time".

My intermittent fasting means that I only eat between 1pm and 7pmish. Other than that, I stay well hydrated during the day and drink decaffeinated coffee and tea.

Hydration is probably the most important part of a healthy body. And it's free, well, my water rates are £34 a month. You need to drink at least two litres of water a day, three if you are exercising, and this can be in tea, but not caffeinated coffee. Water will clean you inside and out, important for crystal clear skin, your digestive system and brain function.

Clean Eating

I wanted to touch a bit more on clean eating, as I found re-learning about food key to my relationship with food. I have discovered beautiful clean food which means I am more than happy ordering a grilled salmon with teriyaki sauce and vegetables than a juicy burger.

My extreme clean eating detox lasts a week or as long as you can manage and very simply put you cut out these seven things. Alcohol, caffeine, meat, acidic food, gluten, sugar and dairy. What does that even leave I hear you ask?! Plenty. Eggs, tofu, brown rice, vegetables, rice noodles, blueberries, pear, papaya (low in acid and natural sugar). It only lasts one week and is a huge reset for your body. In the one week I lost ten lbs, or recently I did it for three weeks and lost one stone.

You then slowly start to reintroduce food like white fish, chicken, turkey, oats and see what feels right to eat. I learnt that my body cannot handle fatty food (I had my gall bladder removed in 2016, gall stones had formed resulting from 20 years of bad, unhealthy food and weight issues), my body doesn't really like dairy, although a cheese board every few months does no harm. Meat is tough on my digestive system, can take weeks, months to process.

If you want a healthy body reset, this process is worth doing!

Colonic Therapy

I also discovered the world of colonic therapy. A great therapy for cleaning out the digestive system properly from toxins. The intestinal tract is very long; it curls up inside your body and food can often get stuck in nooks and crevices. And stuck for months. A good internal cleanse rids the toxicity. I have one when I feel I need it, normally once a year. It is not painful in any way, and you feel amazing afterwards, and two pounds lighter.

Vitamins

I have got into the habit of taking vitamins daily in 2020. What you take is very personal to you and your needs. E.g. magnesium is great if you're struggling with sleep. Zinc is great for protecting your system from viruses. Vitamin C is great for your immune system, Vitamin D is great to add some additional sun energy, also great for someone like me who suffers from Seasonal Affective Disorder, due to a Vitamin D deficiency. Arnica and turmeric are great for internal healing if you have/had internal fat inflamed organs.

Exercise

I was very fortunate to have a personal trainer for a couple of years recently. It is the best type of targeted exercise I have ever done, I won't dwell on it, it is expensive (£35 to £40 an hour here in Hertfordshire). But I was the most toned and strong that I have ever been in my life after personal training.

I love to do free YouTube tutorials, HIIT with Joe Wicks, Yoga from the PsycheTruth Yoga and wellbeing channel. I go out running, walking miles and bike riding. Lockdown was revolutionary in reminding me of the power of daily exercise and free at that. I ran, biked, or walked 400km in May (and raised £600 and counting for Grief encounter at the same time).

Beauty

I love my beauty products and do love a bright lippy, as followers on my Instagram (@mrsmummypennyUK) will know! I have tried every brand going and I can tell you for a fact that expensive does not mean better in beauty!

The Aldi moisturiser for £7.99 is brilliant, it does the job. As do their make-up wipes, facial cleanser, and glycolic acid toner, get them every three months when they appear for the special buy. Also, their make-up is great too, I have tried mascara, under eye concealer, lipstick, eye shadow, BB cream, eye liner, in fact I have tried everything. I am grateful that most of this was sent for me to try and to pop onto YouTube, but it is very inexpensive. £2.99 for a mascara or lippy etc.

The Aldi Lacura products are also cruelty free and many are vegan, but do check the labelling for the vegan mark, as it is very tricky to create vegan mascara, for example. The only one I have found is Kat Von D, go Big or Go Home, at £20, very expensive, but also VERY good.

Action - Listen to Your Body

My key closing message for this chapter is basically to listen to your body. It tells you when you are thirsty, hungry, or tired. Eat the right food, drink enough water, and go to sleep to the land of dreams where your body repairs and processes everything you learnt that day. The body resets during the night and every day is a new day filled with new excitement and challenges.

More importantly, listen to your body when you feel something is medically wrong. If you find a lump go straight to the GP, if you are bleeding too much every month, go the doctors, if you have extreme stomach cramps go the GP, if you feel extreme anxiety and that your life is spiralling out of control go to the GP.

Can you tell I have had experience of all those things? Unfortunately, the 20 years of not caring properly for my body has given me a few issues but I am so grateful to our NHS who have always done their best to help me cope with or fix my medical issues.

A Page for Your Chapter 9 Notes

Chapter 10 - Making Money – Ways to Supplement Your Income

I want to close out the final chapter of Part 1 of my book sharing some insights into money-making schemes. Budgeting can get you so far but sometimes the reality is, you need to find new avenues to make some cash. This is an easy area to make mistakes in – and I should know.

I debated about writing this chapter in my mind many times and what to include. I have tried it all, which is important to let you know. This is what allows me to write with honesty and authenticity in this section. Most of the money-making schemes that you read about on the internet are too good to be true.

They either take ridiculous amounts of time to earn £10 or they drag you into a dirty, uncomfortable world of online money making. So here is my honest view of great things to make some extra money which might be just what is needed to transform your financial situation. This part of the guide aims to help you navigate painlessly which schemes are worth giving your time to and which you should, in my tried and tested experience, avoid!

Selling on eBay, Facebook, Gumtree

One of the easiest and quickest ways to make some extra cash is to sell unwanted things from your home. I have tried them all with some success. I have sold branded clothes and bags on eBay and made hundreds of pounds. I have sold bigger items such as furniture and toys on my local Facebook Market Place (no fees!).

We all have stuff that we haven't used for ages and a good de-clutter helps you locate these items to get selling. eBay is so simple, especially when you use the phone app. Give a great description of your item with lots of pictures and detail any faults, unless you want it returned!

I have also set up a stall at a local car boot sale and made £200 from selling our old stuff that we no longer needed. That same car boot sale where I met the lady who has proofread this book!

Mystery Shopping

A method I have done lots of and it can be fun when working with the right Mystery Shopping company. The only one I now work with is ProInsight. I know the founders and management team well.

I have had spa days for free, plus been paid for my views on customer service. I get free food and coffee from Starbucks for writing a customer service review. I even got a three-month David Lloyd membership in return for a series of reviews. It's the kind of stuff I love writing about on my website anyway, so I may as well get free products and service plus get paid for my critique and customer service review. The sign-up details for ProInsight can be found in my recommendation page on my website. https://www.mrsmummypenny.co.uk/the-money-guide-to-transform-your-life-recommendations.

I have tried many others! GSK is good for bank mystery shops, as these pay good money. I got £90 once for opening a savings account with a high street bank. It gets closed after a few days with no effect on your credit records. I also enquired about home insurance with another bank and was paid £70 for an hour of my time.

What I will say is that you must be descriptive in your writing and remember everything. So, write the report or questionnaire on the day of your visit! And take names of everyone you have contact with.

I have also had some bad experiences. I earned £40 for putting up shelving in a big supermarket, four branches, taking me four hours. It was so much hassle, plus I drove around 50 miles between the shops, having to pay for my own petrol. I do not do those kinds of jobs anymore. But I have also got five bags of Aunt Bessie's roast potatoes in return for a five-minute questionnaire, bargain. You must buy the roast potatoes but are quickly reimbursed when you scan in a copy of receipt with your completed questionnaire.

Cash Back – Technically a way to save and make money

I LOVE cash back. I have had an account with TopCashback since I started Mrs MummyPenny in 2013. My current amount of money that I have got back in cash back is £3,500, after seven years of using it! My latest bit of cash back is £13.30 from Shark. I got an extra 7% off my £190 new vacuum cleaner, winging its way to me now.

For everything you buy online, search on TopCashback, everything is on there, I mean everything. See what the offer is and click through to the brands page and buy as normal. I have made lots from switching essential bills. There are always rich switching deals for your mobile phone, broadband, energy, savings accounts, bank accounts. I got £120 when I switched to Virgin Media in June 2019 for example (woohoo-this also means that my contract is up for renewal and I can switch and save again, it's June 2020 as I write this book!).

TopCashback has a great referral scheme where you and a friend both share a bounty when they sign up and use TopCashback actively. This can be £5 each, or sometimes £20. They change it all the time, but I have a lots of friends sign up, and followers, So if you want to sign up use this link and we will both benefit from some sign-up cash.

A warning about cashback is to check that the cash being offered still means that the product or service is value for money and keep a check on the cash back payment. Sometimes they go missing and you have to raise a case with TopCashback to locate it.

Online Surveys

I do not do these. I cannot be bothered. I have tried. 30 mins to earn some points towards a £1 Amazon voucher, yeah you are okay. Would rather put a wash on, cook dinner and fill the dishwasher and I hate household chores!

I had a guest writer do a few tests for me in this post. Take a read if you fancy online surveys to make money, link is in my recommendations page on website. It will not make you much. Just being honest.

Refer a friend offers

Many companies have now realised the power of referral and will reward their customers who recommend them to friends. Normally both the referrer, say me will make money as will you the person signing up. I like this model as it's win-win for both sides. My favourites are:

Octopus Energy – You get £50 for signing up, so do I. Via a credit to our bill.

PensionBee – We both get £50 added to our pension pots.

TopCashback – As already mentioned, you get £5 for signing up, I get £15 (offer varies all the time though!).

LifeSearch – Fab independent insurance broker – You get either £25 or £50 cash back depending on value of policy, I get £50 to £100, depending on value of policy.

Mindful Chef – You get £20 off your first and second orders, I get £20 credit to my account.

Trussle – If you re-mortgage and get a new mortgage with independent mortgage broker Trussle we both get £100 of Amazon vouchers.

All my referral links can be found in my chapter 10 recommendations on my website https://www.mrsmummypenny.co.uk/the-money-guide-to-transform-your-life-recommendations.

If you sign up to any of them, we both receive some money, as this section describes, and you then become a customer. You can then offer the refer a friend offers to your friends, only if you love the service and it saves you money obviously. I use all these products and services and love them!

Making Money Schemes to Avoid

Matched Betting

Most money-making bloggers rave about matched betting (because they make money from the affiliate fees, the fees they make when you sign up and pay monthly charges). Let me share with you from bitter experience, it did not work for me.

Matched betting is a way of making a profit from the free bets every gambling company gives out. It's tax free, risk free, blah blah. IT IS NOT RISK FREE.

I made mistakes and lost money. I also made some money, around £2,000. But at a huge cost. I was drawn into the dirty world of online gambling, particularly online slot machines and became addicted. I started putting my own money into the website every day. 30 minutes of a quick buzz. The colours, the sounds, the repetition, I loved it. £20 a day become £30, then £50. I can tell you with confidence as I tracked all my winnings and losses, I lost £1,000 of the £2,000 that I made.

It is NOT A QUICK FIX way to make money. It drags you into the online world of gambling, why do you think the huge gambling companies allow matched betting to happen?

MLM (Multi-Level Marketing) schemes

Another ranty section. I am very anti-MLM schemes. You will have heard of Tropic Skincare, Arbonne, Utility Warehouse, Avon, the list goes on and on. You are recruited normally by a 'friend' to become a team member. You then must spend a chunk of cash and a ton of time to get the products and start selling them to your friends/network.

MLM companies target me regularly, wanting me to sell their products to my audience. It is always a BIG NO. For me as a potential seller of said MLM product I would make a commission from every customer I signed up/sold to, but the money was in the pyramid. If I were to recruit a team beneath me, I would rake in the money as each customer my team signs up would earn me a commission also. My recruiter makes money from my customers and my team and their customers. It is a pyramid scheme and I feel strongly that this industry needs better regulation.

If it Looks too Good to Be True - IT IS

We all get bombarded by crazy money-making schemes (feels like) on a daily basis. But 99% of them are too good to be true. They often require an upfront investment from you regarding money or time and you will end up losing money, sometimes £'000s.

There are so many pension scams, investment scams, sales scams. And they increase in numbers with time as the dodgy companies get better at technology and accessing private data from the general public like email addresses and telephone numbers.

Never reply, block the numbers and tell or educate people around you to do the same. Particularly older folk who are more susceptible to these scams.

If you are ever unsure of a scam email or message, drop me a message on Twitter and I will look! @mrsmummypennyuk.

A Page for Your Chapter 10 Notes

PART 2 –
THE FUTURE

Chapter 11 - Protection – Otherwise known as Wills and Insurance

At 19 I was left a homeless orphan. I was at university at the time so still effectively living at home during the holidays – the only home I'd ever known. Thankfully, what happened to me is reasonably uncommon, however it is something of a cautionary tale for those of us with kids. The key take away from this chapter is please, please get a will and get yourself some decent life insurance. I know these things can feel daunting but honestly the peace of mind it will bring you and the security you leave for your family should the worst happen are priceless.

The death of my parents

My late teenage years were extremely difficult. Mum died suddenly when I was 16. Two years later dad remarried my step-mum and then one year on he died suddenly. Both mum and dad had unexpected heart attacks. My life fell apart, physically, financially and mentally.

There was a small amount of life insurance and they had a joint will ensuring if one partner died the money went to the other. This was never amended in the short time between mum and dad dying. My dad's will was therefore deemed invalid after he had recently remarried and his estate went into probate.

Mum was 58 when she died. She had had a life of complex illness. She had tuberculosis as a child that took one of her lungs, leading to complications later in life. Her pregnancy at 42 (with me) was a lot for her body to cope with. Soon after she had a hysterectomy, then in her late 40s a cataract operation. She developed angina in her 50s and walking any distance became very difficult.

Dad was 63 when he died. A fit and healthy man full of life. He had recently retired from a life of service at the age of 60. His 42 working years were spent with the Marines, then the Army, and then the MOD as a dog handler (by far his favourite job, working with animals). In retirement he threw himself into sport as a keen cricket umpire and spent every Friday and Saturday night at the British Legion. His sudden death was a huge shock to everyone. He also hadn't rewritten his will after his recent re-marriage.

Dying without a valid will was a huge stress for the remaining family.

We had two funerals to arrange with no idea of what either parent would have wanted. I have very little memories of either, just the music, Morning Has Broken at my mum's funeral in St. Just church. You'll Never Walk Alone and the Last Post with a fellow army comrade bugle (that was traumatic) were played at my dad's in Heamoor church, near Penzance. Even writing this is making me cry. I can't cope with listening to these songs.

My dad's money was frozen intestate, yet the funerals had to be paid for. As incomprehensible as it seems when you're grieving, life carries on after death; the bills still have to paid. It took around nine months for dad's money to be released and as per probate rules at the time and the value of the estate, the entire legacy went to his new wife.

The financial consequences were complex and taught me a valuable lesson about life insurance and wills. Life insurance is an essential insurance for me personally, as a mum of three boys with many responsibilities, namely a mortgage.

Having a will is so important. Where the children go is a huge deal and such an important consideration for my will. I want everyone to know where my money is to go, how I want any valuable possessions split. I want an input into my funeral. I want George Michael and Massive Attack played, I want one huge arrangement of purple flowers on my coffin, everybody wearing rainbow colours and all donations going to Grief Encounter.

Why you should write a Will – now

I have only very recently written my first will. I am embarrassed to admit this. I have three children; I have several assets that would need to be divided upon death but didn't write my first will until the age of 42.

Why did I not sort out a will sooner? There were many reasons, the fear of dealing with my own death and the considerations around the children. There were inconclusive discussions about who would look after them should both parents die at the same time. The will to write a will was there, but still I didn't do it.

I now have a will, which does require a review every time a life event happens, namely a divorce, just to ensure that everything is still as I wish it to be, for example money splits, executors, care of children if anything happens.

Writing a Will is Daunting

The idea of making a will can be daunting, but the peace of mind is well worth the effort. With a will, you can be sure your money, assets and property will all go to the right people when you die. Without one, your personal finances will be much harder to untangle. As much as we'd all like to hope this isn't the case, an estate without a will is often a nasty family argument waiting to happen.

Think about the future

According to the government, you should update your will every five years or whenever a major event in your life happens. So, when you are choosing who to write your will with, be sure to investigate the cost of any future updates as well.

How much does it usually cost to make a will?

If you go to a solicitor, you can expect to pay £150 to £250 for a simple will. If you have wishes, a specialist will might cost upwards of £500 – depending of course on exactly how complicated you need it to be.

You can save a lot of money by making your will online these days. There are lots of different providers who offer an online service but do check out my recommendations section at the end of the book for the company I used.

Consider a couple's will

If you are in a committed long-term relationship, you and your partner can save quite a bit by making your wills together. A couple's will (actually two wills) is usually less than two single wills. That is because the will maker can usually use a lot of the same details in both wills.

A standard couple's will might leave everything to whichever partner survives the other, or their children if they've both died. It can also be used to explain who should look after your kids if you both die at the same time. But the two wills can be completely different if you like!

Choose your executors wisely

A lot of will writing services and solicitors suggest that they should also be the executor of the estate. This can be a good idea – for example, saving your family the stress and bother of sorting out your estate – but the service does come at a cost. So:

- Before you choose a professional to be your executor, check what they usually charge for settling an estate. Some businesses take a hefty 5% percentage of your savings!
- Choose a family member or friend to be an executor as well. This makes it easier for your family to not use the professional if they do not want to.

Whoever you choose to make your will, the important thing is to get it done. You might be surprised by how quick and easy it can be. My recommendation of a great online will writing company can be on my website https://www.mrsmummypenny.co.uk/the-money-guide-to-transform-your-life-recommendations.

Insurance really isn't complex

Really it isn't! In this section I'll walk you through what it is, what different types of insurance might apply to you and the best way of going about sorting out insurance for yourself.

I have always thought that our society uses strange words for things in the finance world. Words that have a power over people and feel quite scary. I remember when I first started out with Mrs MummyPenny and feeling like insurance was one of those words and a product that was very complex to understand.

Of course, insurance is not complex now that I understand it. After many years of research, learning and personal ownership of products I can explain in a simple way. Insurance has been rebranded as protection (which makes me think of condoms but let's set that aside). Protection Insurance very simply put is:

> "protection of your income should the worst happen, be that serious life changing illness or death".

In priority order these are the most important protection policies to have in place. Firstly, life insurance, secondly income protection insurance and thirdly critical illness insurance, if needed.

Life Insurance Explained - A story

One of the financial consequences of my life story is that I have always understood the importance of having life insurance. I knew that when I took out my first joint mortgage, I needed a policy that would pay out a chunk of money to cover my share of the mortgage if I died. I was protecting my then partner. He was the one who encouraged me to do this, explaining the importance. We had a £218k mortgage and took out protection policies for £109k each and wrote in our life insurance agreements that the money would go to each other on death.

Back in those days, the year 2000, the financial industry was less heavily regulated as it is now. My policy was sorted by some greasy haired estate agent financial planner, but, to be fair to him, he did a good job. It was with Legal & General and cost just £6 a month. I took out a policy to cover £109k on my death, to last for the 25-year term of the mortgage.

The cost has never changed in the 20 years of having the product. It has five more years left before it runs out. The mortgage on that house and the boyfriend are long gone, but I still have that bargain £6 a month policy, giving me reassurance that I have a good amount of protection in place if the worst happened.

I have recently taken out a new additional policy to cover me for additional mortgage borrowing after my divorce. Despite my substantial knowledge on protection I would never just sign up to a policy with some random company or cold call. Go to the reference section for my recommendations of a trusted insurance company to help you out.

Why Do you Need Life Insurance?

Nothing in life is certain, except death and taxes. A quote that can be traced back to many authors, including Daniel Defoe as the first, in 'The Political History of the Devil' in 1726. We are all going to die and having life insurance in place will ensure that things are easier to organise after the inevitable.

I have life policies that will cover my outstanding mortgage plus a bit extra should I die. This means that my children will have a fully paid-for house and some money left over to pay for my funeral and for themselves. My latest life insurance policy lasts the length of my mortgage.

If you don't have dependants and own your house outright and/or have investments/pension money held in other places that more than cover your outstanding debts, then life insurance might not be necessary. But for most people it is, if you want to protect those left behind after your death.

Things to think about with Life Insurance

There are a few things to consider with life insurance, Firstly, the amount of cover you need, as it is just as important to not over-insure as to under-insure. The term or length of the insurance should ideally match the length of your mortgage. Do you want level cover, as in cover that stays at the same value for the whole policy? Or do you want reducing cover that goes down as your outstanding mortgage balance does the same?

I decided to opt for a £200k policy at £22.98 a month. This lasts for 27 years and is level cover, meaning the cover is

£200k for the full term of the 27 years. Obviously, all insurance is health and age dependent, at the time of taking the policy I was 43, a non-smoker, healthy, with just one little blood disorder (low platelets) to complicate the policy slightly.

The life insurance policy has been placed into trust, which simply means that the money is separate to the pot of money or estate upon death and the beneficiaries of the money receive it a lot quicker to allow them to pay for the funeral. Ensure that this is set up when you take out your life insurance; your provider should help with this.

Income Protection Insurance – Priority Number Two

Employee Rights vs Self-employed Rights

When you work happily (or not so happily!) for someone else as an employed person you have some security. You have rights to notice pay and sick pay, there are statutory minimum rights here, do check with the government site, details in the reference section. As an employed person it's worth just checking with HR what you would be due. Maybe it's one-months' notice pay if you were made redundant. Or maybe its one-month's sick pay at full salary, two months as half salary. Do check your benefits.

I can talk from personal experience here. I have been made redundant twice and have worked for a company that went into administration.

The redundancies were simple, my notice pay was paid and was taxable income, I worked my notice in my last redundancy with EE, as we parted on very good terms. Plus, I received a tax-free redundancy agreement lump sum.

There are statutory minimums here, again check with the government website in my recommendations page on website.

I have taken time off sick. I had a long period away from work at Tesco with mental health issues. I was very fortunate to have full pay sick leave for six months. I say very lucky as the statutory minimum is significantly less than this.

If your sick pay or redundancy pay options fill you with fear, and you recognise that it will not be enough for you to pay your essential bills, then it's worth thinking about Income Protection Insurance.

It is even worse for those of us self-employed, freelance, zero-hour contract people. If I am unable to work, my income pretty much stops. What if you are a painter, and you break your leg? If you are a hairdresser, what happens if you are diagnosed with cancer? What happens if you have mental health issues and need to take a few months off work? Income Protection Insurance is very important for self-employed people.

I first heard about income protection around 15 years ago, but I ran, in fear, at the cost quoted of £180 per month! Many years later I discovered it again. One of the ways I've made sure over the years to keep myself educated about all things financial has been to listen to advice given by fellow money experts and podcasters. Listening to the wonderful Pete Matthew's talking on his podcast about Income Protection, suddenly it became crystal clear to me that this was something I had to have.

- My essential bills would be covered after a three-month period that my emergency fund would cover.

- The roof over my head would be safe if I could no longer earn due to illness.

The Quote Customer Journey

I decided to investigate the cost of this insurance and spoke to an independent broker. For a recommendation of a broker go to chapter 11 reference section. Like the life insurance discussion, you can use the same company to investigate income protection insurance.

You need to think about the following:

The level of cover you need.

You go through your income and expenses. The value of my proposed monthly cover was calculated at 75% of my expenses total. I could make cutbacks if my income stopped; this felt comfortable.

How much emergency money do you have in place?

This is important because it helps you to understand how long you can delay claiming against the income protection. The longer you can delay the cheaper the premium. Three months felt comfortable for me, as I have more than this saved in my emergency fund. Had I set the term to one-month delay on my Income Protection Insurance, the monthly premium would have doubled in price for me.

How long do you need the protection in place?

At what age do you think you will start drawing from your pension? This is likely the age you would run your policy until. The premium is guaranteed, and the benefit is indexed as well, meaning that it grows with inflation price rises.

Your medical history

Height, weight, lifestyle, any illnesses, operations and medical history of my family. This was a bit of a spanner in the works for me as mum and dad died of heart attacks aged 58 and 63 respectively. Also, my brother had a stroke aged 59 (he survived). Serious illness and death before the age of 65 does impact some protection policies and at the very least will raise your premium. Equivalently, that kind of family history makes it more important to me to have this protection in place.

Your independent broker will know the best protection policies based on your exact circumstances. My policy costs around £30 per month for £2500 of income protection cover as a reference point for you.

Critical Illness Insurance – Priority 3

I will not spend too much time on this insurance area as life insurance and income protection insurance are more relevant and important. But this is also an option for certain people. It is a policy that will pay out a lump sum on diagnosis of certain critical illnesses including cancer, motor neurone discase etc. Income protection does the same, but in contrast it pays out a monthly amount until a stated point rather than a lump sum.

Have a conversation with an independent insurance broker, they will help you understand whether this is a form of protection that applies to you. Check out my recommendations page on my website for a great cash back offer from LifeSearch.

A Page for Your Chapter 11 Notes

Chapter 12 - More on Savings

In part 1 we looked at the importance of having an Emergency Fund in place. In this section I want to share with you some insights on how you can transform your life from a 'just about managing' approach to money to one in which you are thriving. By thriving, I mean no longer tempted to take out debt, but in a position whereby you have savings that give you options to do those things you've always wanted to do.

Medium-Term Savings Option – Savings for 1 – 5 years

If you want a higher interest rate and you are keen to leave your savings in cash (and not take the risk of stocks and shares) then a fixed term savings product is a great option. These products are a great option when you are saving for something fixed in the not too distant future. Maybe a new car in three years' time or some house building work in two years' time, or maybe even a holiday of a lifetime for your family to Disneyworld.

Each of these products can be set up for your children also if you have something short term in mind for a child. If the children's savings are longer term, then I discuss this in the next chapter- investing.

Regular Saver

The regular saver product is where you save a regular amount each month for a year and you receive a better rate of interest. These are normally limited to £250 per month or less and the bonus interest is paid at the end of the year. Just set up the direct debit and leave it for 12 months, then pull out the money with the bonus at the end of the 12 months as the interest rate will revert to practically nothing at the end of the year.

Fixed Term Savings

There is also a fixed term savings product, where you save a bigger chunk of money for an agreed period. Maybe one year, two years or five years. The interest rate offered is fixed for this period and there will be penalties for withdrawing the money early. You must be certain that you can lock this money away for the period agreed.

Lifetime ISA (LISA)

This is a great way to save for buying your first home. The account can only be opened between the ages of 18 and 39 and must be used either to buy your first home or left for retirement or you will pay a penalty for withdrawing early. You can save up to £4000 per year and will receive a £1000 bonus for each £4000 saved, 25%. A few rules, to get the bonus. The house purchase must be your first anywhere in the world, you can only withdraw money after one year, the house being purchased must be less than £450k. Couples can have one LISA each.

Cash ISA

You can save your money in a cash ISA, the benefit of this is that you can save up to £20k a year and all interest earned is tax free. However, for basic rate taxpayers, the first £1000 a year of interest received on your savings, whether ordinary accounts, fixed term or regular savings, is tax-free, known as the Personal Savings Allowance. Higher rate taxpayers can earn £500 a year in interest tax-free.

All my product recommendations can be found in the recommendations page of my website.

A Page for Your Chapter 12 Notes

Chapter 13 - Investing Your Money

There are other ways of making your money work for you – ones that are riskier but bring higher returns than any of the more standard savings account options discussed in the previous chapter.

Investing is an interesting issue – and a gendered one. Did you know for example that just 23% (source of statistics on recommendations page of website) of female adults in the UK hold an investment product, compared with 35% of men?

What I hope to do both through my company Mrs MummyPenny and through this book is empower women to take charge of their money more – including peeking into these less well-known aspects of the financial world such as investing.

That said, my own journey into creating my investment portfolio has been less proactive initially than you might imagine, so I understand the reticence many people feel when thinking about stocks and shares.

My Investing Story

I started my corporate career aged 22 with HSBC. I was in the product finance team producing reports on the profitability of bank products to HSBC. It was a great job; I learnt so much about every banking product and how the banking system really worked.

In the first week I needed to set up a HSBC bank account to ensure I got paid and at the same time I set up a stocks and shares ISA. The woman in the HSBC branch near Pudding Lane was great, I remember the conversation well; she explained the benefits of the product to me, I understood the risks of investing and the potential gains. I opened the product and set up a £25 direct debit for every month.

Every month my £25 went into a HSBC fund, a mixture of the top 500 companies in the world. I was buying very small bits of shares in companies like Tesco, M&S, HSBC etc. It was a well-diversified fund with all industries covered and all countries represented. I left that direct debit set up for 14 years.

Age 36 I needed the money to partly pay for the house extension and withdrew it. I had invested cash of around £4k and the investment was worth £8k after 14 years. I had doubled my money. This felt great.

I experimented with buying individual stocks whilst on maternity leave. I had a little bit of spare redundancy money and I wanted to learn something new during my time off with my first baby. I researched companies and tried to calculate company shares which were undervalued and would maybe go up in value.

I made some good decisions and I made some mistakes. I went big with Tesco shares, and bought £2,000 of shares only for them to lose 50% of their value very quickly after the financial crash of 2008. My big learning was, not to play with stuff that I didn't really understand.

I am now more than happy to invest my medium-term money into mixed, balanced, ethical funds. I am happy for institutions to manage that money for me and watch it grow over time! A warning that I must point out, investments can go up as well as down.

What is Investing?

Investing is very simple in concept, you buy a little chunk of a company, a stock or share, that rises or falls in value every day on the world stock exchanges. With this comes risk, the risk that the shares value might go up or down. To mitigate this risk, you put your money into a group of shares or a fund.

Investing in stocks or shares (S&S) is different to saving in cash. When you save your money into a cash savings account, you will be given an interest rate of say 1%. If you save £1000 you will get £10 interest during the year. With stocks and shares the return is not guaranteed. There is the risk again that the value of your initial investment might go down, or the return that it might go up.

Women in general invest less than men. Why? Women are more risk averse and are brought up with the belief from influences like friends, family, media that investing is for men. IT IS SO NOT FOR JUST MEN. Investing is simple and you can start saving from as little as £10 a month. You can choose exactly where you put your money, in groups of companies (funds) that match your personal beliefs.

My view and my view only, but I have always seen a better return on my S&S money than I ever have in cash. I produced this graph for some work with a client.

Let us look at a monthly investment of £25, £50 or £100 for 20 years. I have used a prudent assumption of 5% annual return. 5% is really very low, often the annual returns on investments are higher.

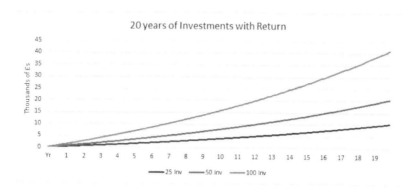

20 years of Investments with Return

A £25 monthly investment after 20 years is worth just over £10k. This is a good return based on total contributions of £6k. But just look at the impact of investing £100 per month! The money is worth £15.5k after 10 years and £41k after 20 years. I could have been sat on a pot of £41k after 20 years of investing.

This is a perfect demonstration of compound interest in cartoon format from @instachaaz from a Zopa Bank campaign (printed with their permission). The longer you invest or save means greater returns. A perfect way to explain to younger people about the importance of starting that savings/investing journey as early as possible. But also, it is never too late to start.

A Stocks and Shares ISA

A S&S ISA is the ideal place to invest your money. A tax-free vehicle where you can invest up to £20k per tax year. This £20k is a combination of cash and S&S ISA, you can have both, but they must not exceed £20k per year. Most of us are fine with the £20k limit!

You chose your S&S ISA provider; a list of my recommendations is on my website. Once you choose your provider you chose the funds that you would like your money invested into or chose a selection of funds. Some investment company will help you choose with very clever questionnaires to determine your risk profile and what your requirements are in an investment. ISAs have the big advantage that unlike pensions you can whip money out whenever you like, and your withdrawals won't be taxed.

What to use your S&S ISA money for

As I mentioned S&S ISA's are for medium-term savings, and my personal investments are for my children. In five to ten years they will all reach 18 and I want to have a chunk of money ready for them to do what they choose with. Maybe a deposit on a flat or help with university or some money to help set up a business. Whatever they want to do, there will be a chunk of money for them to help at the age of maturity.

You can also invest money in Junior ISA's in your children's names, into cash or investment ISAs. I have these for my two eldest children, partly funded by the £250 voucher the government provided when they were born for child trust funds, that I have topped up. This funding stopped in 2010.

This money then passes to them when they turn 18. It depends how much you trust that your children will manage the money effectively at the age of 18, I guess?!

Other Investment vehicles

There are many other products that I could talk about. In fact, so many that I could write a whole other book about it. These products are for people with a lot of money, with more than £20k each year to invest. I am not writing for that minority. If you do have that sort of money to invest regularly, I would suggest it is probably prudent to talk to a financial planner.

A Page for Your Chapter 13 Notes

Chapter 14 – Long Term 10 years and beyond Pensions and Financial Guidance

Pensions are another one of those issues that we all know are important but generally we're a bit rubbish at taking the time to fully understand and sort out.

I think especially if you're a busy mum (is there any other kind?) the last thing you want to do once the kids are in bed is sit down and figure out what your long-term financial strategy is for that hazy futuristic time when you no longer go out to work. There's a sense that, well there's always the state pension, and of course since the government's introduction of the auto enrolment of employees into company pension schemes, there's a tendency to think, or hope, that it will probably all work out for the best. I hate to break it to you, but this is dangerous thinking.

This section is all about helping you to access the shortcuts that are out there to really sort out your pension and get some security in place for your future that you'll only be thankful for in the long run.

My Pensions Story

The biggest financial regret of my life is that I didn't start a pension saving scheme until I was 31. I spent every penny of my £40k+ salary in my 20's – buying designer handbags, having great nights out and trips away with friends, going on holidays. It also got spent on more 'sensible' items such as the mortgage, car and putting away some savings but at the end of every month I was cleaned out.

Opting out of my pension contributions during my 20's was not the smartest financial move I've ever made. That £100 per month, which would've been matched by my employer, would be worth circa £50k now in the pension pot. Ouch!

I'm not proud, but I did it because my philosophy has always been that life is for living. Being touched by the death of my parents at such as young age I was conscious early on that life is fragile and a one-time deal. I wanted to spend my 20's living my life experiencing amazing things, eating at the best places, shopping luxe items, which is exactly what I did. Those were extremely happy times and I cherish the memories enormously.

After the birth of my first child when I was 30, I began to take life more seriously. I started contributing to my pension upon returning to work after maternity leave, I had two employers in my 30s and managed to put away a nice chunk of money with them contributing as well. By the time I left the employed world I had around £30k in my pension pot.

When I became self-employed my pensions contributions stopped. One of the biggest downsides of self-employment is the lack of a pension scheme to join and an employer making contributions when you do. When I started Mrs MummyPenny, I was not earning enough money; pension contributions fell way below paying the mortgage and buying food.

I consolidated my employed pensions early self-employment into a new fund with lower fees with PensionBee. I was also able to contribute to my new pension pot whenever I chose to. I restarted my contributions from my company after I had been trading for three years.

I am looking forward to moving my pension money to the Fossil Free Funds next. I am incredibly passionate about where I spend my money on a day-to-day basis and I want to do the same with my pension money. Just imagine the impact if we all moved out money away from companies who are doing great harm to the environment.

Your Pension Options

State Pension

The state pension builds from contributions to national insurance. It becomes payable later in life. This age can change based on government decisions and is expected to change in the future. For the latest retirement age for men and women visit the government pension website as mentioned in my recommendations page on my website.

You need to contribute national insurance contributions for 35 years to be eligible for the full state pension. Again, you can check your contributions on the government website. This is key for women to check as you may have gaps when you have had years out of work. Another inconsistency for women is that during maternity leave years you may have a significant national insurance gap. Check your own record and have the knowledge. If you reach retirement age with say 25 years of the 35 in national insurance contributions your state pension will be reduced. It can be topped up by you or your partner at any time before retirement.

It is very unlikely that the state pension will be enough for you to survive, the government is even saying this. It is advisable that you start paying extra into a pension, whether a work pension or a private pension such as a self-invested private pension (SIPP) from as early as possible.

Employment and Auto-enrolment

If you are employed pensions are a no brainer. Your employer is giving you FREE money. For every chunk of salary that you pay into your pension, your employer will be doing the same. Every employer is different, but they must at least put in 2% for every 4% that you save. The pension contribution is taking from your pre-tax earnings and is an auto-enrolment. Auto enrolment is about employers signing employees up for a workplace pension, unless the employee chooses to opt out. It is FREE money, why would you opt out?

Your employed pension is accessible younger than the state pension, currently from age 55 at the earliest. Again, this age can change with government policies so it's best to check with your work pensions provider. Most likely though is that if we are still working in our 50's, it is sensible to leave the pension money until you definitely need it for living expenses.

Self-employment and Pensions

Inevitably, pensions are trickier as a self-employed person. But setting up a good pension scheme that works for you is totally doable. Maybe you are like me and have a few pension pots dotted around, and you can consolidate them with PensionBee and then add to it as and when you choose. Or you can set up a regular transfer. It totally depends on how regular your income is. Mine is very sporadic, so when I have a good month, I put money into my pension, when it's not a good month, I do not.

The great thing about pension is that you get tax relief. If you are self-employed you can include your pension payments on your tax return. And if you are a higher rate taxpayer, it will reduce your tax bill, you will need to include it as an expense in your tax return to reduce your tax bill. Or if you own a limited company your company can contribute into your pension for you, reducing your corporation tax payable. If you are a higher rate tax band payer this is well worth doing!

Other Types of Pension

Of course, you do not have to have a private pension. Many finance experts suggest different ways to manage your money. You can invest in property or stocks and shares ISAs as an alternative. I would always suggest a balanced approach is good - it makes sense not to put all your eggs in one basket. Spreading your money around a number of different options to diversify your risk and return reduces the likelihood of you being held at the mercy of, say, a state pensions crisis or a massive financial markets crash.

Overall, pensions are a very tax efficient way of saving, as either the money is deducted from your earnings before tax is taken off, or your pension company adds the tax relief. The money is locked away for, potentially, a long time but it's totally worth it – if the worst should happen to you before you die, don't forget that you can name your loved ones on the policy ensuring they can benefit.

Spending Pension Money

When you decide to spend your pension savings, the first 25% is tax free, but the remaining money is income tax payable. There are many considerations here about pulling your money out and annuities (that pay an income each year), at this point I suggest it's a good idea to speak to a trusted financial planner. It's likely to be a significant chunk of money that you need guidance with.

I am a few years from this point, and to be honest, I don't intend to draw down any of my pension money until my mid 60's. At that point I will review with a financial planning expert.

Financial Guidance

We have a strange financial guidance and advice system in the UK in my opinion. Shockingly if you have between nothing and £100k, (yes £100k!) you are unlikely to be able to get financial advice from either an adviser or a financial planner. It would not be worthwhile for the advisor or financial planner to work with you due to the fees they would earn.

A financial adviser can advise you on products to move your money into, and they take a fee from your investment pot and the money you make. A financial planner takes a more holistic view of your life, what you want from it now and in the future, and recommend products based on your requirements for the remainder of your life. They guide you into how much you need to invest or put into your pension to generate the income you want in later life when you might want to stop working. Typically, the adviser takes a cut of what you make, and the planner charges an upfront hourly fee, like a solicitor.

I prefer the financial planner route and have included a trusted firm on my recommendations website page There are also free sources of information including the PensionWise for the over 50s planning retirement.

If you fall between £0 and £100k then you are likely to have to fend for yourself. This very book gives you the basics plus other books and ways to learn that I recommend in the reference section. It isn't right or fair that financial guidance comes at such a cost, but that is the state of financial management in the UK: money talks.

A Page for Your Chapter 14 Notes

Chapter 15 - Do What Makes you Happy

How many of us are stuck in jobs because we feel we must stay for the pay? That 'doing what you love and getting paid for it' is merely a pipe dream, or something that can only work out for a few lucky ones?

I've been there. Trapped in jobs that I didn't love, that drained me of all my energy and spirit. Jobs that I was tied to for the money; living an existence in which money controlled what I did. Sure, I had the sense of being able to buy and do things I wanted, but all from within that prison of working to someone else's orders.

It really doesn't have to be that way. In this final section, more than anything, I want you to think about how else you could be living your life, how undertaking the changes outlined in this guide could really help to put you back in control of your money and lead to the transformation you most want and deserve.

My Story: From Rat Race to Choosing My Own Pace

One Monday morning I found myself sitting on the tube rumbling towards Paddington in London with tears streaming down my face. I was shaking with anxiety about having to go back into a workplace that didn't light me up. I was overweight, tired, drawn. Juggling the job, the kids and never feeling like I was doing very well at either of them. Worse, I couldn't feel who I was anymore in the push/pull of everyday existence. And that was my reality – existing. Sitting there, in the cold harsh light of the tube that Monday morning, realising that in a minute I'd have to sort my mascara out and pull myself together, again, I decided there had to be another way.

I wasn't going to be beaten by a system that wasn't built by me or for me. I was determined I would carve out a way of living and working that was based on joy. Something I have worked towards, achieved and continue to build on now. The philosophy of my twenties hasn't changed, life is for living now and we've only got this one life, so I'm determined to seek every day to make it the very best it can be.

My last employed role broke me. I had three small boys at home who were spending more time with their childminder than with me. Everything was a rush; I had no time to myself, let alone for my boys. The commute into London was a killer. I was not looking after myself physically, hugely overweight and drinking too much alcohol. Then the bullying started. A manager told me to choose between my job or my family. As always in these crisis moments I chose my family.

Eight months later I left EE with a mutual compromise agreement. I walked away with enough money to pay my bills for the next 18 months, leaving me free to tend to my fourth baby, Mrs MummyPenny, a girl.

There it was, the perfect storm of a business that I had already set up as a hobby and some money to pay the mortgage whilst I built it up to a good earnings level. I did it properly. I got an enterprise grant from the government, one of the pre-requisites was that I wrote a clear business plan. I took advice from expert business mentors who all offered their time for free. I hired an accountant, set up a limited company, business bank account and had a lawyer friend available when required.

I went for it. The first year was all about writing content and networking. I made very little money. The second year was much of the same, but the income started to roll in and brands were noticing a new (ish) personal finance expert who spoke with honesty and authenticity. I made some money in year two. The business has grown consistently each year with profits growing by around 50% each year.

I love what I do. My business is me and I am my business. And I am incredibly grateful that I took the risk and set up my own business. Every day I get up and love what I do. I have flexibility to work hard when I need to, or to take it easy when my boys are around or when I need to decompress and self-care.

I get to learn so many new things, meet incredible people and help to shape exciting new businesses as well as my own. I am part of the team with my key partners and I have financial freedom. I call the shots with my business; I decide who to work with and who not to work with. And now after a few years, am trading successfully and am working towards financial freedom as well as having savings for beautiful holidays every year.

Self-employment is not for Everyone

Self-employment is not for everyone. Many people prefer to work for an employer, hopefully in an industry that they are passionate about. The benefits of working for a large or small business are wonderful. A pension contribution, holiday pay, sick pay, maybe free coffee, or a gym, or incredible work travel trips or a sailing trip along the Solent (I did this when I worked at EE, it was incredible).

The important difference for me was around control. Control is one of my core needs and I was always very unhappy when I have had a controlling boss or worked for a controlling company. Likewise, I was happy when a few bosses gave me free rein to do whatever I wanted and would always do the best job ever. I can only remember maybe five good bosses who ever treated me like that out of many. And you can rarely choose your boss!

When you run your own business it's you that totally calls the shots. You control every day, every decision and your destiny.

The corporate world was a huge struggle as a mum and as a woman with strong views. I was deemed aggressive and emotional, if I had been a man I would have been described as assertive and passionate. I spent so much time at work and never felt like I was giving what I could or should to my children. With my own business I can be the real me and be as in control as I want to be and as emotional as I want. And decide where my time is spent. Business, children, self-care, friends.

If I want to write, or speak about an opinion piece, I can do what I want (within legal writ boundaries!). If I want to record a podcast or a live social media video and cry in it, I can. If I want to rant about issues that I feel passionate about, I can. I love this. No one can mute my voice.

The Side Hustle

We all have something that we love doing that we could monetise. Maybe you are an incredible cleaner and love doing it, maybe you can bake, sew, paint, sing, design, care for animals or people. The list can go on and on. I have so many friends who have realised their life passion, their personal and business passion and have merged both. They are making money from doing something that they love.

The side hustle starts as exactly that. Something you do on the side of your regular job. As it was for me, Mrs MummyPenny began two years before I quit my day job. You do need to build up some savings and financial security before taking a leap unless you have a partner or family or some other financing to back you up.

And if it all goes wrong, it does not matter. You still have your day job to fall back on. You will make mistakes and fail. I have made so many mistakes, very expensive mistakes, but I have learnt from each one and become a better businesswoman and person as a result.

Life is about balance. Save for the future and enjoy life today. Do what you love.

A Page for Your Chapter 15 Notes

Chapter 16 – Don't Just Take it from me, Take Guidance from other Experts in the Personal Finance World

I am very grateful to have many knowledgeable and influential friends in the world of leadership, personal finance and coaching. I asked each of them what are their top short-term and long-term personal finance tips they wanted to share.

Romi Savova – Founder and CEO of PensionBee.

(My business partners since 2016, and who look after my private pension)

My top short-term tip would be:

Put whatever you can into your pension as soon as possible. Few savings vehicles are as attractive as a pension: the government gives generous tax incentives and it is easy to find good value, diversified investments online, including through PensionBee. The power of time is your most valuable investing tool and it is absolutely free - the earlier you start, the longer your pension will have to grow and the more it will benefit from compounding returns (the returns on your returns that are automatically reinvested without your having to do anything at all).

And another one:

Consolidate your pensions as regularly as necessary, starting now. The average person will have 11 different jobs in their lifetime and almost all these jobs are likely to come with a pension that benefits from employer top-ups in addition to your own contributions. Through consolidation, you can get your retirement savings in one place, with one balance, one straightforward way of contributing and eventually, one easy way to withdraw. You would never leave your bank account lying around and unchecked, so apply the same discipline to your pensions. A pension provider like PensionBee can help you take control and make you pension confident.

And finally the long term:

Invest some time in finding the right pension provider for you. Then after you have consolidated your pensions and decided how often you wish to contribute, leave your investments alone. Don't be tempted to regularly switch investments unless you have a very good reason for doing so, for example you want to make your savings more ethical. Your pension will likely be invested in the market - a basket of global company shares and other financial instruments that are traded daily. Therefore, your balance will go up and down; that is part of long-term investing. Ride it out so that you can reap the rewards. If you take your money "out the market", for example by placing it into a cash fund, you are very likely to miss out on investment gains and future you will miss out on valuable pension income.

Pete Matthew – Founder of Meaningful Money & Director of Jacksons Financial Planning and fellow Penzance friend.

Short term

The best financial tip I can give anyone is to try to build an emergency fund. Easily the most frequently received comment in my inbox during the COVID-19 pandemic has been 'thank goodness we had an emergency fund in place'. Having 3-6 months of your basic monthly outgoings in a bank account you can access immediately gives incredible peace of mind. I know it might sound like an insurmountable task to get that kind of money together, but it's hard to put a price on that kind of security, and it's SO worth the effort.

Long term

The biggest headwind working against you in the long term is compounding. That sounds nuts I know, because that same power is very much ON your side when building wealth. But compounding works in reverse when it comes to costs.

When investing and building wealth for the future, there's a lot you can't control, such as markets and the economy or whether your chosen fund manager is having a good year. But you can control costs, and that includes tax. Look to shave as much cost as possible off things like your investment ISA or your pension and save tax by using those tax efficient products. Every penny you pay in charges on these accounts and others is a penny which cannot compound for you in the future. Make your money work for

YOU, and not your financial adviser, investment manager or anyone else.

Faith Archer, Personal Finance Journalist/Broadcaster and Founder of Much More with Less Website (and personal guide to me on my finances and budgeting)

Short term

My number one tip for the short term is to keep a spending diary. Jot down everything that you spend, so you can see where your money disappears and make changes. Just knowing you'll have to write it down can stop some spending in its tracks!

Long term

Then focus on how small changes today can make a massive difference in the future. Thanks to the magic of compounding, making small overpayments on your mortgage, or paying regular amounts into your pension, really add up over time. I'm looking forward to choosing when I retire, rather than being forced to work till I drop. Your future you will be so grateful.

Jordon Cox, AKA 'The Coupon Kid' and Founder of Jordon Cox.com Website

Personal finance tip for the short term:

Whenever you're online shopping and about to buy something without looking for a voucher - STOP! Nearly every website has a 'voucher code' section where you can get money off your basket - so that means they are out there.

Before you press 'buy', do a quick Google search for that retailer and 'voucher code'. You might get lucky and score some extra money off you weren't expecting.

If there isn't a voucher code, have a look on cashback websites where you could get a percentage back from your purchase.

Personal finance tip for the long term:

So many Brits are scared to speak up when something is wrong. The only way companies can improve is through customer feedback, and on top of this, you're usually compensated for things not being up to standard.

It's not being picky - remember your consumer rights! Things must be to a satisfactory standard as described - and if it's not, tell them. Common examples are incorrect meals at a restaurant, stale or faulty food you've bought from the supermarket and dirty hotel rooms. All these complaints can result in freebies for you, helping your pocket too - and it's always something to remember throughout your life.

Kat Byles, Founder of True Business, that leads with your creative spirit and honours your heart.

Short Term

Use your money consciously to create the world you want to live in. If there is a choice, I will always use my money to support women in business, to support local farmers that don't use chemicals. I love the relationships this creates, the emotional investment in their success. I have stopped giving money to Amazon as I don't support their business practices and instead am finding lots of lovely other companies to buy from directly.

Choose to save for something you'd love. This makes you conscious of money going out that could be better spent on what you'd love, while inspiring you to explore ways of increasing your income. Start by saving what you can - even if it's a fiver, start.

Long Term

Choose a financial income intention that opens inspiration. Not a figure that you think you can create such that it feels dull and not one that is so ridiculously outlandish that it is fantasy. Choose the financial figure that opens inspirational flow and gets your subconscious mind creating the jackpot financial structure that will create that figure. You'll receive a whole lot of energy, enthusiasm, creative development as well as your financial income intention.

Clare Gambardella Chief Marketing Officer of Zopa Money

Short term

Have a look at a breakdown of your spending in an average month and have a view on what you could save by making a few changes, whether it is to spending patterns, subscriptions or providers. There are lots of apps that can help with this or a good old spreadsheet or note pad will do the trick. Then open an instant access savings account and move the amount you want to save into that account at the start of each month or as soon as you are paid if your pay isn't monthly.

This will help because it takes the money out of your current account balance – making it less likely that you will dip into it for ad hoc spending. However – the easy access nature of the 'savings' pot means if you do need it for a good reason – there is no hassle. See how much remains in the easy access account after a few months and if you feel confident enough – move it into a fixed term account where it can earn some interest.

Long term

ISA allowances are my long-term top tip. Use your allowance wherever possible. ISAs are great as they help you to save tax free. There are lots of different types from cash, to stocks and shares and innovative finance ISAs, so you can find a good fit for the time period, return and risk that you are comfortable with. While these are a great way to save for the long term, they can also normally be accessed if needed along the way - so that gives you some peace of mind.

You might also consider a Lifetime ISA if you are between 18 and 40 years old. These are available from some online providers and are designed to help people save for a property deposit or for later in life, You can use a chunk of your ISA allowance for a LISA and the government will match your investment, up to £1000 per year until you are 50, so it can be a great deal.

Acknowledgements

This is the book that I have wanted to write since I was a little girl. My life has taken many twists and turns, some amazing, some incredibly destructive and insufferably sad. I knew that I wanted to share them in a book. The time is right, the time is now.

I dedicate this book to my mum, the strongest woman I ever knew. She was only in my life for 16 short years but made a huge impact.

She taught me anything was possible. That education was important, that anyone and everyone was welcome in our house, that the beach and sea are a perfect day out. She taught me the value of working for a living, how to make Bolognese and rock cakes, how to cross-stitch and repair a hole in anything. She taught me about flowers, birds, animals, how to do the laundry in the twin tub and peg it to the line after the spin cycle.

Her spirit passed to me on 26th June 1993 and I forged ahead to achieve so much. A maths degree, a qualified accountant, a list of the best jobs, three beautiful boys and a hugely successful business, Mrs MummyPenny.

Thank you, mum.

The biggest thank-you to my troop of angels who have supported me so much in recent turbulent times.

To Bec, who has been there every step of the way since we were eleven, my soul sister. And who only bloody edited this book and coached me through some of the more challenging moments. She has coached me through my entire life. I quote her writing on my 40th birthday photo book.

> " What followed (becoming friends) were boyfriends, bad decisions, crimping and dyeing hair, mixing all the spirits in the drinks cabinet just because, Chesney Hawkes, sausages and chips with your mum, periods, bras, exams, "Forever", heartbreaks, laughter and tears through the good times and the tragic and the bloody-awful-should-never-have-happened times. We became #friendswhoarefamily."

To Neilboy, Anita, Fran and Marianne who have been around forever, it feels like. Always there for wine, holidays, coffee, miles of walks, spa days, Newcastle 'work trips', being stranded in London at 6am, Ibiza, burgers, Vegas, cocktails. Everything I love, with the best guidance, encouragement and support like you would not believe. My angels and my cheerleaders. Friends really are family.

Finally, leaving the best till last to my boys, Dylan, Josh and Jack, who are the reason I do what I do. Enabling us to have financial freedom and time to enjoy growing up together.

Thank you for reading, here's to savings much money and your financial freedom.

Lynn Beattie is the founder of Mrs MummyPenny Ltd.

You can contact her on

Lynn@mrsmummypenny.co.uk

Subscribe to my Weekly Newsletter on

Website - www.mrsmummypenny.co.uk

You can follow her on

Twitter - @mrsmummypennyuk

Instagram - @mrsmummypennyuk

Facebook - MrsMummypenny

Facebook Group - Mrs MummyPenny Money Saving Tips

YouTube - MrsMummy Penny

Podcast - Mrs MummyPenny Talks

LinkedIn - Lynn Beattie ACMA